Prints In The Valley

By the same author:

The Sugar Factory
The Pleasure Within

Prints In The Valley

ROBERT CARTER

SECKER & WARBURG
LONDON

First published in Great Britain 1989 by
Martin Secker & Warburg Limited
Michelin House, 81 Fulham Road
London SW3 6RB

First published in Australia 1989 by
William Heinemann Australia

British Library Cataloguing in Publication Data
Carter, Robert, 1945– .
Prints in the valley
I. Title
823'.914[F]

ISBN 0-436-08814-2

Typeset in 12/13pt Garamond by Bookset Pty Ltd, Melbourne
Printed in Australia by Macarthur Press Pty Ltd

This work was assisted by a Writer's Fellowship from the Australia Council, the Federal Government's arts funding and advisory body.

Between the dreaming and the real there is no line.
They are of each other as the air and the sky.
Who denies the one or the other, has scratched out his eyes
and cut away his tongue.

Inscription, Haus Tambran, Kinduli, 1968

PART I

1

Australia 1963

From the party on the second floor, Elvis Presley's voice slips through the plywood door and trembles down the stairwell.

Ah found a new place to dwell,
it's down the end of lonely street . . .

Alec follows his friend Miles up the concrete steps, unconsciously climbing in time to the music. He is sweating. They arrive at the door with Alec's left foot on Elvis's *Heartbreak*. Miles passes the carton of beer he is carrying to Alec as he knocks on the door. Alec feels uncomfortable and wishes he had not come.

The music is too loud, as the door opens and dumps cigarette smoke and beer smell over them. The party and the flat belong to Ross Iverson who will be married in two days' time. Ross sits on the floor in the middle of the room: John Wayne surrounded by savages. Alec takes the beer to the kitchen, acknowledging the whoops and cries of greeting from the drinkers. Elvis feels so lonely, he could die.

Alec levers the top off a bottle and pours himself and Miles a glass of Resch's Pilsener. He sits on the wide, padded arm of the lounge. The round, ropey cord of the upholstery edge presses into his legs.

Waterloo, Waterloo,
where will you meet your . . .

The record is scratchy.

'A toast to Roscoe.'

Glasses in the air.

'To the gloom-to-be . . . I mean the groom-to-be.'

Laughter.

'To the bedding . . . I mean wedding.'

More laughter.

Everybody has his dayee
everybody has to payee . . .

'Do you know the facts of life, Ross?'

'Does Bronwyn — more to the point.'

'More to the point . . . aha!'

Laughter.

Alec shifts his feet in discomfort across the floor. The carpet has swirling roses and autumn-coloured leaves. In the corner of the room, a Kreisler television with a control knob missing balances on spindly, pointed legs. An imitation wood-grained buffet with sliding glass panels touches one side of the set. Behind the glass is a sprayed-gold coffee set with tiny cups and twirling patterned jugs. At the far end of the room, double doors open onto a small balcony bounded by black wrought-iron railing and two pots of sickly geraniums.

Alec has come for Miles's benefit. Ross Iverson is a friend from their high school days but, unlike Miles, Alec has never maintained the links.

Ross is drinking too much. He is expected to drink too much. He is white-skinned, thin and tall enough to keep himself stooped in apology to most other men.

The Morley twins, Ian and Phil, nod in time to the music. They smile a lot and rarely ever complete a sentence. Alec believes they have developed an internal language that makes it difficult to communicate with others. Ian had tried to explain it to him. He said that to talk to someone besides his brother meant that what was understood between them had to be explained so patiently that within a few mouthfuls of words it didn't seem worth the bother. Alec liked to watch them sending signals to each other with a twitch of the mouth or an eyebrow — like cardsharps.

Alongside the twins sits red-haired Trevor Burridge, smoking a pipe which repeatedly goes out. Trevor sucks until the spit-rattling noise causes someone to stare or pretend to tip beer down the bowl. And there is Stafford Mitchell who doesn't have a job at the moment, or any other moment that Alec knows about. 'Stuff-it', he was known by at school. Once, not long after they finished high school, Alec sat in the back of Stuff-it's car. A green Morris Minor given to him by his father, the town's only baker. He was the only one of them to have a car and he used it, Alec thought, in lieu of a personality — to reward and punish. On Alec's last day in the Morris, Stuff-it pulled into a Caltex service station, filled the car with petrol, checked the oil, all by himself, waved to the grateful owner, and drove off without paying. Alec was horrified. He slapped Stuff-it on the back of his head. Stuff-it laughed, and the other two in the car said nothing. Alec and Stuff-it had an almost-fight, pushing each other and yelling. Stuff-it was broader and stronger than Alec but, as everyone knew, had an annoying fear of him. Alec might do anything. He had never been seen in a fight, so who knows? And there was something else about Alec that Stafford didn't want to think about. Dion was roaming

around and round and round
he was the kind of guy who'll
never settle down.

Stuff-it unveils his projector and dirty slides. He begins closing the venetian blinds. With his two fists of iron, Dion is going nowhere.

The fan in the projector hums as the lens is aimed at the eggshell-coloured wall. A naked woman with a breast held in each hand is fired onto it. The circle of men respond with calls that are expected of them, and another slide is loaded. A laughing, half-dressed woman with eggshell-coloured teeth is draped across a motor bike.

Ross is being shown, by his friends, the things that marriage would take from him. A ritual meant to signal his movement towards the enemy; a celebration of how those that were left were not afraid that their circulation could so easily be throttled by a tight, gold ring.

On the wall, two black girls are helping each other to

expose the bright pink parts between each other's legs. Ross is swaying and looks as though he will pass out from the drink. He is given another. Crash Craddock has a girl

who is so fine
he loves to hug and kiss her
all the time
and in the evening
when the lights are low,
he watches his boom boom baby go
a boom boom . . .

Stafford runs through his worn slides again. This time the viewers are quiet, respectful almost, intimidated by the persistence of the naked women. Alec wonders whether another run through the slides might huddle them together into the furthest corner of the room.

The venetian blinds are pulled up, and light takes over the room. No one looks at anyone else. Alec can feel the effect of the alcohol. Bronwyn, Ross's wife-to-be, has supplied jatz biscuits covered with slices of boiled egg, or cheese and tomato. They eat in silence. Elvis says it's okay to burn his house and steal his car.

While Trevor is in the toilet, one of the twins crushes a jatz biscuit and stuffs it into the bowl of his pipe. Everybody laughs approval. Miles leans over to whisper to Alec.

'Stafford says he has a ball and chain in his car, and we should chain old Roscoe up outside Bronwyn's.' Alec shakes his head.

'Count me out.'

'Naked,' Miles says with a laugh. 'So he'll have something to tell his grandchildren.'

'With Bronwyn's fox-terrier, he mightn't have any grandchildren.'

Trevor strikes his fifteenth match, patiently heating the jatz biscuit. Miles turns the record player off, and the radio on. He turns the tuning knob.

'I have a dream,' says the negro voice. Miles continues turning the knob until he finds music.

Alec walks out onto the balcony. The night is clear. He looks at his watch and calculates how soon he can leave without offending anyone. Inside, he can hear Stafford returning with the ball and chain. There is a loud cheer, some yelling and scuffling. Alec wishes himself away. Beneath him, on the street, a girl in white shorts, blouse and tennis shoes steps out of a car. She has a white cardigan draped across her shoulders. She swings a tennis racquet in an exaggerated arc, gracefully, and laughs along with the driver of the car. She walks around to the driver's side and leans in the open window. Alec imagines they are kissing. The girl pulls her head back out of the car and quickly looks up and down the street. It is empty and she laughs with appreciation of her own daring, and relief that no one has been watching. The driver starts the car, touches her face with his hand, and drives away. The girl stands waving to the shrinking car. From inside the flat, Ross lets out a yell. The girl in white looks up. Alec is caught staring down at her. She is embarrassed. Alec smiles reassuringly at her. She raises her racquet to blot Alec out, and runs up the driveway to her house.

Miles is tugging at his arm. He drags Alec into the living room. Stretched across the lounge, semiconscious, is Ross — dressed in a too-short, nylon floral dress. One ankle is encircled by a thick, rusty chain with a heavy metal ball on the end. Everyone is laughing, except Ross who looks pale and ill.

'We have to get him down the stairs yet,' Stafford giggles.

'We could just roll the ball down, and let him go,' Miles jokes.

'Or toss it over the balcony,' Stafford shouts. 'Come on, we'll carry him . . . get hold of his legs . . . and his ball . . . ha ha ha . . .'

'It weighs a bloody ton.'

'Jesus, Alec, you could help.'

Alec doesn't move. 'Why don't we leave him here?'

'There wouldn't be any point.'

'You've made your point.'

'Come on, we'll leave him on Bronwyn's lawn.'

'Leave him here,' Alec says.

Stafford lowers the top half of Ross Iverson back onto the lounge.

'You're a bloody miserable bastard,' he says to Alec.

'And you're a dickhead.'

Stafford controls his swaying as if part of his drunkenness has been an act of cooperation. 'You must want a smack in the head.' He stares at Alec.

'You seem to have already had yours,' Alec says. Miles raises his hands and steps between them. 'Come on, come on you two — let's have another drink, this is Roscoe's last night, remember.'

'He's a bloody spoilsport.' Stafford waves a beer glass at Alec.

'He's a moron,' says Alec.

Stafford lunges towards Alec with the beer glass, striking him on the bridge of the nose with its thick base.

'Jesus, shit,' says Miles.

Blood from Alec's nose spurts over his lip. Alec shakes his head and sprays large drops across the sleeping Roscoe's dress.

Stafford leaps towards the door, wrenches it open and jumps down the concrete steps four at a time. Alec runs after him, catching his foot on the steel carpet-edging of the doorway. He sprawls headfirst, arms outstretched, down the steps, rolling over and over, cracking his head against the concrete, over and over. Buddy Holly says, that'll be the day.

And Alec is flying. He glides and dives, spins and rolls, slipping through air and cloud, higher and higher. Ascending past sky, where the air becomes thin and cold and the ground falls away — a leaking, muddy balloon. And still higher. Past anything, past everything. Until there is God. Smiling. Smiling at Alec.

'I have a dream,' Alec says.

'Ssshh, sshh, I'll go and get sister.'

'I have a dream . . .'

Alec tells God that his dream is stronger than everything.

'It's your soul, Alec,' God says.

'Is it all white?' Alec asks.

'Of course,' God answers.

'With blue suede shoes?'

'Mr. Glover, can you hear me?'

Alec asks God to wait.

'Mr. Glover, open your eyes, I know you can hear me.

You've had a nasty fall, but you're all right now.'

'One great thing . . . one great thing, God.'

'Alec, it's Kate, can you hear me?'

'Kate?'

'Yes.'

'God looks like Elvis.'

'He'll be all right, dear, don't worry, he's not quite awake yet. Mr. Glover, open your eyes. That's better, isn't it? Do you remember falling down the stairs?'

'Kate?'

'Yes, Alec?'

'I have a dream.'

'Yes, Alec.'

'One great thing.'

'Should we get the doctor, sister?'

'I want to do.'

'No need to talk, Mr. Glover, just open your eyes.'

'One great thing.'

I am the master of the dream and you are a caretaker. A listener caretakes a dream passed lovingly through time as his seed.

Under care of its keepers, the dream fades and flourishes, collecting possible lives as real as children.

I speak from within man's dream of himself; of the mosaic of paths that are laid for him and by him; of man who sees his own death, and dreams beyond. For I am the Tambran and I am everything: I am master of the dream, and trace, with love, your prints in the valley.

2

New Guinea 1967

I sit in the haus-meri to watch what the two old women do to my friend Mennen. One is Sakalin, the first wife of Wahgi, and the other is Wakuli, a fool who stays to be beaten by her husband instead of returning to her line. I have heard her cries in the night. Sakalin's eyes carry hate when she looks at me, and I know it is because her husband has looked on me. He has looked on me from before my breasts were grown, from when I was a picanini — and I would like to tell her this. I do not turn away from her eyes, and more so, I raise my head so that I am taller. But inside, I do not feel this strength. I would not have Sakalin at my opening.

Mennen is afraid, I can hear her heavy breaths and she holds her own arms so that her shaking will not be seen. I have been told by the old meris what must be done. I feel afraid for Mennen and think that it would be better for me to be in her place, as I am stronger.

Mennen had her first blood on the day of mine, and we were sent to the haus-moon together. The old meris told us of the men's fear of our blood and how it is a poison to them, that when we bleed we must never step across the cooking pots or straddle the stream or give food with our hands. There are stories that the old ones fill our heads with, stories of how, in the hidden anger with their husbands, they would pass between their legs the hot kaukau taken from the fire. And they would watch it go down the mouths of their husbands. Some of them would get sick, and some of them, when they were told what had been done, would never come back to their wife's house. The old ones laughed and teased and boasted about the days when their skin was soft and there were young and fearless lovers waiting high up on the wall of the valley, past the garden fences. Hungry young men who could not wait to taste their bodies.

Sakalin holds a thick stalk of tanket leaf. It has been heated over the fire so that it can be bent, but will not break. Wakuli leans against the inside of Mennen's leg and forces the other one apart with her feet. I can see Mennen's opening. Sakalin unfolds the opening to pink, holding each side with her spread fingers, and twists the tanket stem into Mennen. There is a skin inside that must be broken, for it has poisoned blood in it, and the opening must be stretched in preparation for the man who will be her husband, who already brings payment for her.

I feel as if the tanket stem and Mennen's pain is inside me. I want to pass water but I would not leave her yet.

I think that when Mennen goes to the Lagaip village with her husband, I will be alone except for Suli. The others are stupid and I will not spend my time on them. Suli was born in the year before me but he and Mennen and I have always run together. Suli is the only one of our line who goes to the mission school and he learns the talk of the Europeans. He wears the clothes of the white men, and he tells us many of the words and of their secrets, and of their God, who he says they pinned to pieces of wood. I have not told Suli yet, nor my father and mother, for they are too sick — but I will go to this school with Suli.

My parents are sick with pig-bel from the sing-sing at Poragali. My father no longer eats, and my mother's food comes out of her mouth again and lies in a stink on the dirt floor of the house. I am happy to leave them and run into the bush with Mennen and Suli, but each day, and at night, I cook for them and I want them well again.

My father is not one who stays in the men's haus, he has always chosen to sleep in our haus and he has told me many secrets of the time before the white man. He does not beat my mother and he does not buy a second wife, even though he has the kina and pigs.

I have spoken to a newly married woman called Gabi who comes from Tambul. She was working in the garden of her husband's mother, and I saw that she was crying. I am not one who walks past such things, and I ask, even though I know I should not, what it is that she cries for. She does not speak to me at first, and I sit down and wait. I have some pandanus nuts in my bilam which I take out and offer to her. As I chew, I see that she is no older than me, her breasts are the same size as mine and we are neither one taller. She has a kina shell and some beautiful neck cords which would be gifts from her husband from the time before the marriage, when he would want to win her. She talks to me of her line, many days' walk away, and of her mother and friends. She tells me of the time before the marriage when she was free from working the gardens and could run with her friends and go to the haus-kundu at night and tease the boys — and laugh and dance and sing. She dreams at night that her body alone remains in the house of her husband's mother, that her spirit has returned to her village, where it holds hands with her friends as they sing the songs of their child-days.

I see Mennen begin to fight and kick out with her legs. Wakuli sits on her stomach. Mennen calls out my name to help her and I stand and ask Wakuli to get off her stomach. Sakalin spits on my foot and orders me to leave the haus. I am confused. I feel the wet of the spit run between my toes. I am trained to follow the orders of the married women. My eyes leave those of Sakalin, and I can see that the tanket stalk has not been heated enough — that it is not soft and does not bend enough. Sakalin watches me as she stretches Mennen's opening. I lean towards Wakuli and grab her ears and begin to pull her off Mennen. Sakalin spits in my face. I pull harder at Wakuli's ears. One of my eyes is filled with Sakalin's slime. She hisses at me; her teeth are brown with chewing betel nut and her curses stain the air between us. With a sharp thrust, she pushes the stem hard into Mennen, who screams and sinks her teeth into Wakuli's back.

Wakuli leaps into a corner whining and clutching at her back. Sakalin is grinning, pointing the blood-red stem towards me. I do not care about the poison, I shut my fingers and swing my hand hard into Sakalin's face.

There will be a price to pay for this, I know, but my swinging arm is fed by the fear and pain of Mennen, Gabi, and myself. And for some moments the pain is turned around.

3

Australia 1963

The blackboard says it is Wednesday. Alec sits at the back of the classroom watching the short, fidgeting boy in the front row. The boy is not listening to the teacher, who is talking and pointing to the blackboard which has chalk drawings of Aborigines eating kangaroos and witchety grubs. The boy is bouncing up and down in his seat by flexing his buttock muscles. Occasionally he shifts his chair on the floor so that it makes a wooden shriek that slices through the teacher's sentences. Most of the windows are closed to keep out the noise of highway traffic and the blinds are drawn to block the Sydney sun. The room is like a brown paper lunch bag, huffed full with breath and ready to burst.

Alec has told the teacher not to respond to the boy's behaviour while he is observing him from the back of the classroom. He wonders why the teacher doesn't bear with the noise and open a window. The boy stands up and looks directly at the teacher for correction. When nothing is forthcoming, he is momentarily unsure, like an actor missing a cue. He looks around the classroom and sees Alec watching him. The boy smiles and Alec involuntarily smiles back. The boy tips over his chair. The teacher's talk is bludgeoned by the clatter, but she persists by holding up a picture of an Aboriginal bark shelter of half-moon shape that reminds Alec of the corrugated iron migrant hostels at Warwick Farm. There are two Aboriginal girls in the class, and the teacher, Miss Benton, seems unaware of this as she proceeds relentlessly through her lesson.

The boy at the front is now crawling on the floor under his desk. His back is lifting the desk up and down. He pretends he is looking for something that he has dropped. The red-haired boy sitting next to him begins to twist and jerk in his seat. The teacher tells the red-haired boy to sit still. Alec can see the boy on the floor curling his pencil around the red hairs of the other boy's leg, and snapping them out with a flicking movement of his wrist. The red-haired boy reaches down and finds his attacker's nostril with his thumb and index finger. This brings the boy jetting upwards from the floor, so that his head crashes underneath the seat with a masonite-cracking sound.

The teacher looks to Alec for guidance. Alec strides down to the boy, picks him up and carries him outside, swinging from his waist like a reluctant dog. There is a look on the boy's face that says the script has been resumed.

'Are you the counsellor?' the boy asks.

'Yes.'

'What are you going to do with me?'

'Break your legs off and beat your head in with the stumps.'

The boy laughs. Alec puts him down and feels a shot of guilt for letting his need to be liked usurp his role.

The school counsellor's office is also the sports equipment storeroom. From time to time, a student arrives to get a soccer ball or cane hoops or to return cricket stumps and bats. At the far end, there are two old, wooden public service chairs, where he sits with the boy. The boy finds it impossible to sit still — he fiddles with the buckles on the cricket pads and looks in all the cardboard boxes. He accidentally pulls one over, spilling tennis balls plomping and hopping across the floor. He quickly looks at Alec's face, which remains neutral.

'It was an accident,' he says.

'I'll help you pick them up.'

As they crawl across the floor in search of balls, the boy talks. His name is Jacques because his father is French and his mother is Swiss, but he refuses to be called anything but Jack, except by his mother. He wants to play football, but is too small and every time he is allowed to play, he is injured and carried off the field. He is clever at reading and drawing, but not at mathematics. His best friend is David Johnston — with a 't' — but not always. Sometimes David Johnston has somebody else as his best friend and Jack waits for his turn. David is big and plays football in the front row, and he is not afraid of anyone or anything. Jack is not afraid of anyone or anything either, except sometimes the man next door, and his mother when she is angry, and the headmaster, Mr. MacLachlan, because he canes you twice on each hand, and in winter the cane makes blue lumps, like grubs, across the tips of his fingers. Jack is not afraid of the cane. When he comes back into the classroom and they all know he has been hit — the boys, and some of the girls, even, look at him differently than before, as if he had been coloured-in like a blank page of his botany book. Jack always makes sure he walks slowly across to his desk, as if the headmaster were a minor interruption to his day. He makes sure that his eyes have been washed clean and dried in the toilet block beforehand.

Jack has an exercise book at home that he keeps at the back of his wardrobe, behind the shoes, in which he does drawings and writes stories. His favourite story is called 'The Two Boys Who Went to War'. The two boys are best friends; one is called Tom and the other is Bill. They are both very strong and afraid of nothing. One day, at the front line, they run out of ammunition and the Germans capture them. They are marched across deserts and old battlefields in straight lines and they mustn't talk to each other or a guard will come and prod them with his bayonet. They are always very hungry and thirsty and tired, and there is a lot of talk in their heads which can't get out. One day, Tom and Bill decide to escape. They make a break for it out of the line of marching prisoners, but Bill gets shot in the shoulder and Tom, who could have made it to freedom by himself, comes back for his friend and the guards smash their rifle butts into his fingers as a punishment. Bill's wound begins to get worse and eventually Tom decides to cut the bullet out. He has an old pocket-knife that he has been hiding in his shoe, and he uses it to cut out Bill's bullet.

With the bullet out, Bill's shoulder heals, and Tom's fingers get better. Then one day, they realise that they have come to the end of their journey. There is a huge barbed-wire fence with guards with machine guns and German shepherds, and they are marched through an enormous gate. On the other side there are holes the shape of giant tin cans dug in the ground, so that each prisoner, when he is placed in a hole, can only see above the ground for one second if he jumps up. Food is passed down into the holes and a bucket for the toilet is emptied every day. If anyone tries to climb out of their hole, the guards can shoot them in their heads. One day, Tom decides to dig with his pocket-knife to try and find Bill's hole. At night, he digs and scrapes away at his tunnel, flinging the dirt out and away. Each day he sends a little dirt out with the toilet bucket, and after many months, his tunnel breaks through to another prisoner's hole. But there is no one there. Tom decides to keep tunnelling in search of Bill's hole. Each night he works harder, and some weeks later he crumbles through to another pit. There is no prisoner in this hole, either. Tom wonders why there is no one in the hole, but begins work on a tunnel in another direction. Sometimes Tom thinks he hears the Germans laughing about him, and that they actually know about his tunnelling, but he doesn't let that stop him.

Jack has not finished the story yet, and he doesn't know how it will end. At home there is just himself and his mother. His father lives with someone else. His father was in the war in Indochina, against the Vietminh, and he too was wounded. But that was before Jack was born. Every second weekend he stays with his father and one day his father is going to come back and live with him and his mother, but not yet, he is not ready yet. Jack's mother is called Anik, and she has black hair like his, and works for a French agency that translates films and newspaper articles. Sometimes Jack goes with her to work and watches the films.

Jack asks Alec what he is going to do with him.

'I don't know,' Alec says.

Jack thinks about this and says, 'Miss Benton doesn't like me.'

'I'm not surprised.'

'Me either,' he says. Alec laughs. 'She sends me to the headmaster.'

'I'm not surprised.'

'Me either,' says Jack. Alec laughs again. 'Do you play football?'

'No.'

'Why?'

'Because I'm no good at it.'

'I'm going to play in the school team next year.'

'I have to talk to your mother, Jack.'

'She works all day.'

'I'll phone her at work.'

Jack's mother meets Alec at her front gate in the early evening. He knows Jack is at football training. Anik Pendraud is tall and as dark as Jack. The house is a Federation brick, with two long verandahs. Inside, the lounge room has beautiful velvet curtains and Bauhaus chairs, a wall of books to the ceiling and another wall of framed photography and pictures. Alec notices original watercolours and prints of Chagall, Kandinsky and Klee. It is un-Australian, and Alec feels intimidated. He is accustomed to fibro houses with laminex tables and cracked vinyl tiles; to mothers with drooping hair and fluffy slippers; to kitchen cupboard doors with plastic ventilation grids and food stains; to pictures on the wall of horses charging through a stream. And on the sideboard, with the china that is too good to be used, wedding photos in an expensive, silver frame, floating on a white lace doily.

There is strong coffee and thick shortbread biscuits which Alec can't help from exploding down the front of his shirt. He sits on a deep-cushioned, three-seater lounge, awkwardly balancing the cup and saucer. As she leans closer with a plate, Alec smells a strong breath of alcohol.

'You have been kind to Jacques, Mr. Glover.'

'Not really.'

'Oh?'

'I mean, yes, it's my job.'

'To be kind to children?'

'To find out about them.'

'And what have you found out about Jacques?'

'His teacher, Miss . . . er . . .'

'Benton.'

'Miss Benton is concerned about his behaviour in class.'

Alec has said this sentence a hundred times before, 'concerned about his behaviour' — it meant the teacher wanted to have the boy's frontal lobes torn out (preferably while he was awake). This time it sounds false.

'And what is she concerned about, exactly?'

'He makes noises in the classroom which distract the other children and the teacher.'

Anik Pendraud does not touch her coffee, she drinks from what looks like a half-tumbler of spirits.

'Is this all?'

'No, he doesn't seem to respond to correction.'

'What do you mean, correction?'

'He has had the cane from the headmaster, for disobedience, several times.'

'And the cane has not corrected his behaviour?'

'No.'

'Then why does the headmaster continue with it?'

'I suppose as an example to the rest of the class.'

'And not for Jacques?'

'Well, that too, of course.'

'Of course.' Anik leans closer to Alec. 'Why are you here, Mr. Glover?'

'To find out . . . to understand more about Jack.'

'What is there to understand?'

'His behaviour . . . and . . .'

'About anyone.'

Alec stares at Anik. She stands, jerkily over-correcting a slight sway.

'What is there to understand about anyone, Mr. Glover?'

'You might have some idea why Jack is . . .'

'Some idea . . . some idea . . .' Anik Pendraud walks carefully around the lounge and leans against the back support with both hands near Alec's shoulders. 'Some idea,' she says, mocking the phrase. Alec feels his face becoming hot.

'I can come back another time,' he says.

'No, no, I have time taken . . . taken time from my work.

We will talk about some ideas I have.' To his relief, Alec feels her hands leave the area near his shoulders, as she walks across the room and finally sits down close to him on the lounge. He drains his coffee cup and smiles politely. She leans closer, conspiratorially.

'You would like to know of his home life?'

'Well, yes.'

'I don't think it is any of your business.'

Alec is annoyed.

'You have no sense of humour — you Australians.'

'Perhaps I should talk to his father.'

'He does not live with us.'

'Jack told me.'

'And what else has my Jacques told you?'

'Not a lot.'

'Not a lot?' Anik stares at Alec. She places her hand on his leg. Alec knows he should leave as quickly as possible, but he doesn't move. Anik wriggles closer on the lounge.

'Would you like to kiss me?'

Alec can't believe he has heard correctly. He is caught between wanting to laugh it away and the surprising appeal of the woman who suddenly seems to have shrunk to an eager, kissable little girl.

'See, you do not laugh.' Anik giggles as she stands and walks towards the swinging louvre doors leading to the kitchen. 'One moment, please — I shall return.'

'I will have to be going,' Alec says numbly to the swinging kitchen doors.

Alone, Alec shakes his head and lights a cigarette.

'Who would believe this,' he murmurs to the room. Anik returns, swinging through the doors and holding a large black-and-white photograph. She hands it to Alec and leans across his shoulder to look at it with him.

'That is Jacques, he is two, with his father, and of course me.'

'Who is that?' Alec points to an older man at the rear of the group with a perfectly trimmed white beard and proud stance that would have earned him the guillotine two hundred years before.

'That is my father — do you think that I am like him?' Anik steps backward, stands straight and lifts her chin.

'No,' Alec says. 'But your husband is.' Anik takes the photograph. She looks at it once, and then tears it into little pieces, sprinkling them from her palm into her almost empty drink glass. She sits opposite Alec and concentrates on his face.

'We will talk about Jacques. I do have some ideas about him — about Jacques and myself. We are lost — lost souls — and you, you have come to redeem us — like Parsifal, the innocent fool whose compassion has made him wise — you have come to redeem us.'

As Alec is leaving, she stops in front of him, before he can reach the door. He is aware of her shape, a child-like quality, and a faint flesh-like smell he finds attractive. But her face is no longer calm and sure. Alec is uncomfortable and looks away.

'He is not like the other boys — Jacques, no matter that he tries so hard.'

Alec glances once at her face as he sidles awkwardly through the doorway.

'I sometimes wish that he did not exist,' she says. Alec smiles, pretending the comment is light-hearted.

'I'll call you in about a week,' he says.

'You like my eyes, don't you, Parsifal? "Dark eyes, deep heart," my father used to say.'

Driving home, Alec realises he has been sweating as his shirt cools in the breeze from the wound-down window. Jack or Jacques would seem an odd son for her. Jack can't find a balance between himself and others — expecting too much and foreseeing too little. Perhaps the dry Australian heat, like a bushfire mirage, has warped his vision of the space between people — making it appear closer than it really is. But he has learned something, that little boys must only be afraid of fear. 'If you don't cry, I'll buy you an ice-cream,' Alec's father had told him outside Chernich's, the dentist, over twenty years before. Alec could no longer cry — and eventually Jack will not cry.

She had smooth, pale skin that must have been kept out of the sun, Alec thinks. She said that Jack has not accepted that his father is not coming back. Jean Pendraud wants to return to France after they are divorced and she will stay in Sydney. Jack does not know any of this but he is to be told by both parents together, very soon, she said. Who in hell is 'Parsifal'? 'Dark eyes, deep heart' — the woman needs help.

Alec leans towards the windscreen and looks at the clouds huddling in the sky. The traffic rolls and stops, rolls and stops. Tonight he will pick up Kate and they will eat pasta at Marino's and go to the movies. Afterwards they will come back to his flat and perhaps make love, and then Alec will drive Kate home to her shared house at Croydon, because she couldn't bear her house-sharing girlfriend to think she was immoral. And she will not move in with him because her parents are Methodists, as Alec once was.

The first spots of rain blow into the dust of the windscreen. Alec remembers being a Methodist. Sunday school texts: THE LORD IS MY SHEPHERD, I SHALL NOT WANT, printed on postage-stamp-sized cards and stuck into scripture books. At twelve, the idea occurred that having a shepherd turned you into a sheep. He was made to sit every week on the dark-stained timber benches which refused comfort. Miss Hyland would squeeze and torment the organ, while the Reverend Southwell droned and nagged and accused from his pulpit: ROCK OF AGES, CLEFT FOR ME, LET ME HIDE MYSELF IN THEE as the sun struggled to get through the stained-glass saints. OH FOR A THOUSAND TONGUES TO SING MY GREAT REDEEMER'S PRAISE! Drier than dust.

In his mind, Alec would make up different lives for each of the people racked in the pews. He would scratch messages under the seat with his coin for the collection plate. And the minutes would stretch into eternities of space, where feet couldn't run, and arms couldn't throw and voices couldn't be heard.

Underneath the seats, pressed into the corners of the timber, were hardened lumps of chewing gum: generations of children's undigested hours.

4

New Guinea 1967

The Tul-Tul has said that I must work in Sakalin's kaukau garden for two weeks as payment for striking her face. I do not care about such a payment and I do not speak to Sakalin at any time in her garden. The stupid woman has not watched me closely enough as I planted her kaukau and snapped off most of the shoots with my thumbnail. She will be waiting until her teeth fall out before green stems break through the earth.

If my father and mother were well, I would not have been punished so. But I do not care today, for I am with Suli and it will be my first day at the mission school. I have made Suli ask them at the school to take me and they have said yes, that they would like to have a meri come to their school. Suli said that I should ask permission from the Tul-Tul as my parents are too sick, but I do not want my chance of school to be lost. There are only boys at the school and I know that the Tul-Tul will not want a meri to go.

I make Suli wait for me along the track as I must go into the bush to pass my pekpek, which is like water. I have done this three times since waking in the morning. My stomach is afraid, but I am not.

Suli shouts at me to hurry. 'Koam, I have to meet Yamka and Nagi along the track, you can't have any pekpek left?'

'Would you like me to show you?' I tell him.

Yamka and Nagi are slightly smaller than Suli. They wait for him every school day. When they see me from a distance, they begin talking quickly to each other. Suli looks at me, hoping I will want to go home. The one called Yamka points his finger at me and says to Suli, 'Is she coming?'

'Yes,' says Suli.

I nod my head and smile at them.

'She will have to wear a dress,' Nagi says.

'Why will I have to wear a dress?'

'Because all the women at the mission wear dresses,' Yamka answers.

'They are all white women,' Suli says.

'They have to cover their breasts,' Yamka says.

'That's because they have white ones,' Suli replies.

'No, it's because they are breasts. And she has them.' Yamka and Suli look at my breasts.

'It is Jesus who says that Christian women must wear dresses,' Nagi says.

'Will Jesus Christ be there?' I ask. They ignore my question.

'No, it's not,' Yamka says. 'Kwila told me that breasts make Christian men want to be picaninis again and they can't stop thinking about them, and they forget they are men.'

Everyone goes quiet to think about what Yamka and Suli have said. At the front of the track, Nagi stops, turns around and says, 'I think it is so you don't have to wash underneath where clothes go — only where you can see skin.'

None of us believe this and I think to myself that Nagi must find the work at the school very difficult.

In front of the schoolhouse there are lots of boys. Suli stops me running into the bushes again. Misus Kane stands on the steps up to the doorway smiling at the children who come past her. When Suli takes me to her, she puts out her hand and I look at Suli who tells me to hold onto it and shake it up and down. Misus Kane's hand is softer than mine, even though she is much older. It is a hand that has not dug much in the ground or carried heavy bilams. She tells Suli to wait while she takes me to her haus.

Inside her haus, I see many things — it is bigger than the men's haus and it is full of beautiful cargo. She takes me by the hand into a room with a small platform in the middle. When I stare at it, she tells me it is a bed. From the wall she opens a door and takes out a very small dress. She lifts up my arms and pulls the dress over my head. It only comes down to my laplap but she seems very pleased and points to the dress and says 'blouse'. I think to myself that I will correct the other boys when they try to tell me it is a dress. The blouse is beautiful and feels like Suli's shirt. It has colours painted on it and it makes my breasts look bigger as they push the front of it outwards.

In the schoolroom I sit near Suli on a wooden seat which has a table in front of it. At the front of the room, Misus Kane talks English words and makes white marks on the black wall. Sometimes a boy is told to stand up and say something about the marks on the wall. Sometimes the boys put their hands into the air and Misus Kane picks a hand. Then everyone sings a song. I can hear only two words, 'Jesus' and 'sunbeam'. I will have Suli teach me the words after school finishes.

A boy makes a noise by shaking something in his hand. I learn that it is called a 'bell' and that when it makes its noise, everyone must rush out of, or into, the school.

In the middle of the day, Suli and I eat cold taro with Yamka and Nagi. The boys run around and climb things and yell out to one another. I ask many questions and tell them I am wearing a 'blouse' which Misus Kane keeps in her bed.

Back in the classroom again, we are given paper and pointed sticks called 'pencils' to make our own marks. I cannot bring myself to do it; to ruin the white thing lying flat in front of me. I do not know what marks to make anyway. Suli makes the same as the marks on the black wall.

At the end of the day, my head is paining and I am left surprised again as everyone shuts his eyes and puts his hands together in front of his face, while Misus Kane says quiet English words that seem to float around the room. And then the bell is making its noise and the day is over. I pull off Misus Kane's blouse and hand it back to her. She smiles at me and tells Suli to tell me that it is for me to keep.

I wonder what I will have to give for this blouse.

On the way home, Suli tells me the words of the Sunbeam

song: 'Jesus wants me for a sunbeam'. I am worried about this — 'a sunbeam'? I ask Suli why does Jesus want me to be such a thing. Suli has not learnt that yet, but he thinks it must be good.

'Can you be something else?' I ask him.

'What?'

'I would like to be a brown hawk.'

'I haven't heard of Jesus wanting anyone to be a brown hawk,' he sneers at me.

Suli tells me that apparently one day Jesus watched a sparrow fall out of the sky.

'What happened to it?' I ask him.

Suli says that the story didn't say. 'I think it spattered onto the ground.'

'What did Jesus do?'

'He just watched.'

'He mustn't like birds, then.'

I take off Misus Kane's blouse and fold it into my bilam as I tell Suli that I will only wear it at school so that the Tul-Tul will not notice and make me stop going. I also tell him that I want him to teach me more English words so that I can understand Misus Kane. I ask him to explain what happened at the end of the day.

'That's how you talk to Jesus, by putting your hands together and shutting your eyes.'

'Why have you got to shut your eyes?' I ask.

'So you can't see him.'

'But he wasn't there.'

'He's everywhere.'

'I didn't see him.'

'You're not supposed to.'

'Have you talked to him?'

'Yes.'

'What did he say?'

'He didn't say anything. I said it.'

'And he didn't say anything?'

'I don't think so.'

'Has anyone ever seen him?'

'A long time ago.'

'What does he look like?'

'A white man, with long hair and a beard, and he wore a long white dress.'

'A dress? How did they know it was him?'

'Because he made magic.'

'Like the masalai?'

'I think so, only he doesn't hurt anyone.'

'Ha, what about the sparrow?'

Suli tells me to be quiet and he walks faster along the track. The day has been much stranger and more confusing than I had thought. Not once did I think of my father and mother in their sickness, or of Mennen who cares for them while I am gone. When I remember them now, I hurry past Suli so that I can wash them and cook the night meal. My thoughts keep returning to the day; I want to learn to hear English words and to speak them like Suli. I wonder about the white men — Europeans, Suli calls them — I wonder where their cargo comes from and how it is that they give it, and their knowledge, away so cheaply.

5

Australia 1963

'You know I don't like the lamp on. No, not even if you put it under the bed. How ridiculous anyway, a lamp under the bed. It would probably catch fire to some of the fluff under there and we would be burned to death.'

'On-the-spot fine, eh? Straight to hell!'

'You're being silly, Alec. Put the light out. That's better, isn't it?'

Outside, warm summer rain is falling.

'You can go ahead now, Alec.'

'I think I left the car windows down.'

'You'd better go and check.'

Outside in only shorts, Alec looks up and lets the rain fall on his face, like hearing, in the distance, high notes on a piano. Under his feet the grass collapses wetly. For a moment he thinks of asking Kate to come outside, to make love in the rain, on the grass. Then he laughs out loud as he imagines her response.

The windows of the car have not been left down, but Alec doesn't care. He slips his shorts off and urinates on the lawn. He throws his shorts wildly and they catch on the car aerial, making it bow and bend. He feels a surge of playfulness and stamps into the grassy puddles like a defiant child, sticking out his tongue for the rain. He stretches out on his back on the grass and spreads his arms and legs. A delicious sense of wickedness seeps through him. He remembers reading of someone spreading their seed into the earth — Emile Zola — and he thinks the book is called *Earth*. He rolls onto his stomach; the rain strokes the flesh behind his knees and between his legs.

'My God, Alec, what are you doing?' Kate's head thrusts out from the doorway; she has Alec's dressing-gown on. He doesn't move.

'Are you all right? Where are your pants?'

Alec rolls onto his back and points to the car aerial.

'Did you slip? Shall I come out and help you? Alec?'

Kate steps warily onto the lawn. 'What happened? Can't you get up?' She kneels alongside him. Alec quickly loops his arm around her neck and pulls her down on top of him.

'Alec, stop it! What are you doing? You're all wet, stop it!'

He pulls open the cotton dressing-gown and runs his hands down her body.

'Alec, this is not funny. Anyone could see us out here . . . Mrs. Anderson could come out into her yard. Please, Alec, let me get up.'

Both hands pass over her buttocks and press up between her legs.

'Alec, let me go, please.'

His hands are wet from the rain.

'I'm getting cold, Alec. I want to go inside. This is making me very angry.'

Between her legs it is wet and his fingers coil and slither inside her.

'Don't, Alec, not here.' She looks towards the fences on both sides of the yard. 'There's someone coming . . . I can hear someone . . . listen . . .'

Her legs clamp tightly around his hands. Her body is rigid. He takes her breast into his mouth. There is the sound of a dog scratching at the garbage bin next door.

She pinches his arm as hard as she can. 'Let me up, Alec, right now.'

He rolls her onto her back. She jams her legs together and covers her breasts with her arms, pointing her elbows into his chest. The rain is constant. She tries to see his face, but it is too dark.

'I want to go home, now, Alec, please.'

He forces her legs apart with his knee and slips his fingers back into her. He works a finger in and out. She grabs at his hand. He feels for her unprotected breast.

'Don't, Alec. You haven't got your . . . Alec, I don't want to get pregnant.'

The dog has knocked over the bin and is rifling and snuffling amongst the rotten garbage. The smell of rancid meat drifts over them.

She stops her resistance. Her arms flop onto the grass at her sides. Her legs are no longer rigid. Alec levers her legs apart and enters her. She does not move or make a sound; her body, corpse-like, is moved only by his thrusts. Her eyes are shut tight against the rain.

Alec is lost. He feels the rainwater joining him to the ground. He pushes ahead, towards something, keeping in front of a silent emptiness, gaining, gaining. He pushes forward. Underneath him, she moves quickly, and his sperm sprays into the ground. Alec cries out, and frightens the dog at the garbage bin. It crashes across the lid and away down the empty street.

'Were the windows down?'

'No.'

'Whatever took you so long?'

'Aha, desperate are we?'

'Don't be silly.'

'It's cool outside.'

'My God, Alec, you're all wet.'

'All over.'

'Go and dry yourself.'

'Come and get wet.'

'You're ridiculous.'

'I know.'

'You're getting the bed wet.'

'I'm a bed-wetter.'

'You smell like something . . . like . . . like grass or something.'

'Rain.'

'Rain doesn't smell — you smell like dirt.'

'*La terre.*'

'What?'

'French for earth.'

'Go and have a shower.'

'I did — outside.'

'A proper shower, with soap and a towel.'

'You don't want to make love to a dirty little bed-wetter?'

'I'm going to have to go soon.'

'I'll have a shower.'

'I hope it's not raining tomorrow, I hate going to work in the rain.'

'Have you ever heard of Parsifal?'

'God, look at the time.'

6

New Guinea 1967

In the early morning, I sit by my father's sleeping-mat. He is awake. My mother makes moaning noises in her chest as she sleeps. It has been many days since either of them has spoken to me. I offer my father some taro and water but he smiles and shakes his head. His skin has fallen inwards around his bones and he looks as though he is made from sticks and grey mud. I am tired of how they both smell of their own pekpek and they do not get better. My mother thinks that a sanguma, a sorcery, has been used against them. She called for a diviner who listened to her dreams and said that a sorceress *was* responsible. My father did not believe the diviner and neither do I. My mother has not spoken since this time except to tell me the names of those who might be her enemies. Her mind is not clear and at night words tumble from her mouth as if they are shaken loose from her memory. I hear the word 'Kuipa', many times, and I remember long ago her story of him.

Kuipa, the boy who left the pathway of the line and who was met deep inside the bush by a masalai — and who became a collector for the Tambran. And whose voice could be heard calling if you strayed from the track; calling your name.

Suli has told me that he has learned at school that germs get inside the meat of the pig if it is not cooked for long enough, and the germs are what have made my parents sick. I wonder about the germs, which, like Jesus Christ, are everywhere but cannot be seen.

'Koam?'

At first my father's voice is so soft, I think it is only his breathing, and then I hear clearly.

'Koam.'

'Do you want something?' I ask him.

'Mennen talks to me of your days at the mission school with Suli.'

'I am learning about everything they know.'

'You are not the son I wanted, Koam,'

'I know that, father.'

'You are much more.'

I am shocked that my father says this to me — he has never told me this before.

'How am I much more?' I ask him. He smiles at me.

'Perhaps you will learn this also at the mission school.'

I am angry with him in my head for teasing me and not telling me what I want to hear — that I am clever and strong and make him proud. In my heart I love him stronger.

'Perhaps the mission has some medicine that will make us well again?' he says softly.

I know that I should have thought of this myself.

'I will ask them today. You should not talk, go to sleep.'

'Go to school.'

'Go to sleep.'

In the distance I see Suli waiting along the track to school. There is someone taller waiting with him. I try to imagine who it could be and I think that I should turn around and go back but then I remember the medicine.

When I am closer, I see it is Kaio and that he has hold of Suli's arm. Kaio is a man with no wives and few pigs and kina. He is hurting Suli's arm.

'Koam Laman, I thought it was you,' he says to me.

'Why do you hold Suli?' I ask him with my heart thumping.

'He is my bait to catch another.'

I think that I could not outrun Kaio.

'Are you going to the mission school with Suli?' he asks.

'Only to get medicine for my father and mother,' I tell him

as I look into his face and hope that he does not see the lie hiding in my fear.

'I have watched you for three days, you carry mission clothing in your bilam and you wear it every day.'

'Let Suli go,' I say, as deep and steady as I can make my voice.

'How can a meri go to school?' he asks Suli.

'I don't go to school,' I lie.

'Yes you do — and the Tul-Tul will need to be told.'

'My father knows.'

'Your father is too sick.'

'He speaks to me this morning.'

'He will be dead soon, and the Tul-Tul will not let you go to school.'

Now I want to kill Kaio. From inside my stomach it rises up my chest and neck and floods into my head. I would cut open his belly and pull out his hot entrails like the men at the pig-kill. I would smash his head with a rock many times until the bone splits and shatters and his brains run over the ground. He grins at me.

'But I shall give you permission to go to school until your father is well again and I shall meet you here in the afternoon — without you, boy.' He shakes Suli's arm.

'I will not meet you here,' I tell him.

'Then I shall tell the Tul-Tul.'

Suli pulls his arm free and runs off down the track. I swing my bilam at Kaio and he stumbles backwards enough for me to run past after Suli. He calls out.

'I will wait for you.'

In the schoolroom I have begun to understand some of what Misus Kane says. She tells me I am quick to learn and I feel very pleased. At the end of the day I ask her about medicine for my father and mother. She tells me that a little doctor must look at them first to see what kind of medicine they need. There will be one coming to the mission soon with the kiap. I am pleased with this news and rush to tell Suli. He has bought a sheet of newspaper from the mission store to roll his tobacco in and to smoke. I ask him to make one for me and he laughs and tells me that meris don't smoke. I tell him that they do not go to school either and he laughs and rolls tobacco for me.

I suck in deeply and Suli watches closely as water comes to my eyes. The smoke cooks my throat and my chest. I do not throw it away; I smoke it down until my fingernails are hot from pinching it and my lip is burnt — and then I drop it at his feet. My mouth feels as though it has been chewing a burning stump. Suli does not say anything but I know he is impressed.

'You should be a man,' he says to me.

'I am much more,' I say.

'What do you mean?'

'Perhaps you will learn at school.'

'Hah, you would be a longlong man,' he says, rolling his eyes in his head.

'You *are* a longlong man,' I say to him and stagger around in circles.

We both fall into the grass laughing and making longlong faces.

'You will have to go home around the mountain,' Suli says. 'Remember, Kaio is waiting for you.'

'I will not go around the mountain because of Kaio — he is a rubbish man and I will walk across him.'

'He wants to go up you. He knows your father can do nothing.'

'I am not afraid of him.'

'I am not afraid of him, either,' Suli says. 'But I am going around the mountain, in case I have a fight with him. I might kill him if I became very angry — so you could come with me for the same reason.'

'It did not look like you would kill him this morning.'

'I wasn't angry then. Are you coming with me?'

'Yes.'

'He will tell the Tul-Tul about you going to school.'

I know this is true, that Kaio is such a one.

7

I am late from walking around the mountain and I curse Kaio. At my house there is no smoke from the cooking fire coming through the roof. Mennen is waiting for me. I know that something is wrong. Mennen's eyes will not meet mine. She looks at the ground as I come nearer. I think of Kaio and I look to see whether he hides in the bushes near the house. There is no sign of Kaio. I do not know why Mennen has not started the cooking fire. I know that soon she will be gone to her new husband's line and I will have no one to look after my parents. I will be pleased to tell my father that soon the little doctor will come with the kiap, and they will have medicine.

Mennen stands in the doorway, blocking my way. I ask her why she has not made the fire. She does not answer and she does not move from the doorway. I tell her that she will make a lazy wife and that her husband will beat her. She looks up from the ground and tells me that my mother died soon after I left in the morning, and my father died only moments ago.

I do not believe her, and I rush into our house. My mother lies still in her corner and I know it is true for her. I kneel down near my father and put my hands together and shut my eyes as Misus Kane has shown me — to talk to Jesus Christ. I tell him that I do not ask for both of my parents to live, only one of them; that my mother can be like the sparrow, and I want my father to stay alive with me. I tell him that I will try to be a sunbeam and that I do not wish to be a brown hawk. I say to him that I have no one without my father and that he is more than a father to me — and I will be more than a son to him — if my father can live.

I say 'amen' at the end, like Misus Kane, in a soft voice, and I open my eyes and touch my father's face. It is cold and dry and I know that he is dead.

8

Australia 1963

'Mr. Glover?'

'Yes.'

'I wish to apologise for my behaviour to you last week.'

'I don't think it was so . . .'

'It has taken a week for me to summon the courage — I would not have Jacques act in such a way.'

'Forget it.'

'It was unforgivable.'

'Okay, I won't forgive you.'

Silence.

'You are joking?'

'How has Jack been at home this week?'

'He is very quiet and stays in his room much of the time — but he is not a problem with me. Has he been in more trouble with his teacher?'

'Yes.'

'I will speak to him again. Can you help Jacques, Mr. Glover?'

9

Alec reels out of the main office and heads toward the staff room. Talking to the headmaster, he thinks, is like screaming underwater. Alec imagines lying on the bottom of the town's Olympic swimming pool, patiently explaining to Russell MacLachlan Jack Pendraud's behaviour. The words coming out in bubbles — floating straight past Russell's headmaster suit and cul-de-sac brain. And yet Alec is courteous, respectful even. Why is he always so polite and cooperative with people like that? He supposes it is one's upbringing. Upbringing? What was that? Being brought up. Up where? Presumably from down somewhere. Down where? Perhaps a more accurate term would be downbringing. Starting up there — brought down here with the upbringing. 'You'll be taken down a peg or two, young man' — 'soon cut you down to size'. 'Sit still and don't ask for anything — don't put them to any trouble'.

And there was love always trying to catch up with the upbringing.

In the end, you were left with the feeling that if the neighbour's dog bit your hand off, you should apologise for the mess on their rug — maybe even offer to pay for the dog's worming tablets. Alec wonders why he continues to feel like this. Because he wants to be liked? Perhaps. Surely not by everyone? Yes, everyone! Later on, of course, you could always drive over the dog in your car.

Looking out of the staffroom window, Alec imagines the swimming pool conversation with the headmaster:

HEADMASTER
What's the story on the Pendraud boy?
ALEC
Oh, he's . . .
HEADMASTER
Do you know I've caned him three times this week?
ALEC
Well . . .
HEADMASTER
(rapping the side of his head with his knuckles) I think there's no one home, up here.
ALEC
The boy's a bit confused too.
HEADMASTER
In my day he would have been flogged.
ALEC
A nice hanging at assembly could be good.
HEADMASTER
By God, we were so grateful for our education, we could hardly wait to get to school every morning.
ALEC
Must have been a big week.
HEADMASTER
They don't know they're alive — boys like Pendraud. Come over here from a foreign country — probably lived ten to a hut, and ate with their fingers.
ALEC
No, he uses his teeth.
HEADMASTER
Too much money, that's the problem, you know. My mother, God bless her, worked all day, sewed all night — made all our clothes.
ALEC
It's a lovely suit.
HEADMASTER
And my father, my God, my father started work at 4.00

a.m., in the dark, every morning.

ALEC

Burglary has its downside.

HEADMASTER

And we used to work so hard, Saturday, Sunday — daylight to dark — we thought *school* was the bloody holiday. Used to fall asleep at our desks . . .

ALEC

Slept right through the old holidays?

HEADMASTER

Kids today — they can't sit still and listen.

Alec laughs out loud in the staffroom. Several teachers look up from their coffee and biscuits. In one corner sit three primary males, in shorts and long socks and Woolworth's shirts. They have an unhealthy interest in all things sport. Alec knows that this is to make up for feelings of deep-down horror at finding themselves locked into a feminine profession — dealing with small children. They develop booming voices at assemblies, and drive big cars, and always take the cricket bat from the senior boys — for demonstration purposes. And they bowl too fast at stringy legs.

And yet, Alec knows some of them are wonderful teachers, with children who would almost follow them into hell. And occasionally, when he speaks to them, he realises that they may never know the best of themselves.

In another corner of the staffroom, four lady infant teachers unwrap Vita-Wheat biscuits with lettuce and cottage cheese, and speak of their diets and the need to lose weight that is already lost. Out of male earshot, they talk of their men, as neatly sealed as crispbreads and containing as many calories. They laugh together, each one attempting to outshock the others with the antics of her mate.

Alec is aware of how cynical he is becoming; some of them, also, are superb teachers. Was he projecting how he was beginning to feel about himself? Could he too be bundled up and thumbtacked to a sentence: a cliche of his time, of his class, of his easy satisfactions? Alec thinks of the song:

All the chapel bells were ringing
in that little village town

and the song that they were singing
was for little Jimmy Brown.

'Are you seeing Jack Pendraud?'

It is Miss Benton. Alec notices her brown cardigan buttoned to the neck and her habit of looking slightly away from him as she talks.

'Yes, Georgina.'

'Do you know what he did two days ago? He took a thumb-tack from the notice board and he stuck it into the back of another boy's head.' Miss Benton's eyebrows rise in expectation of Alec's horror. She rocks backwards and forwards on the balls of her feet.

'What happened before — had the boy said or done anything to Jack?'

'Nothing, not a word. What do you think is wrong with him?'

'I don't know yet.'

'He's impossible in class — you saw him. I just have to keep sending him to the headmaster.'

'Yes, I know.'

'What else can I do? He won't be quiet for a minute. I don't care if he doesn't do any work, but he stops everyone else.'

'Perhaps you could form some small groups, and give them some interesting things to do.'

'Oh, I don't think that's his problem. He just won't ever do what he's supposed to.'

'What about giving him something to do by himself, a project or something?'

'I'm not going to make him special, until he learns he's just like everyone else.'

10

The heat from the sun is beginning to wriggle up from the tar on the airport apron and radiate from the opened metal hangars. Anik Pendraud sits in the car alongside the corrugated iron aero-club building, reading the *Saturday Morning Herald*. Jack follows Alec, puppy-like, towards the plane which is chocked on the grass, fueled and waiting.

Hatches secure, harness tight, trim set for take-off, oil, fuel, etc., etc. Alec never remembers everything on the check-list, or any list for that matter. Once, a long time ago, he was chosen for a school play — but had to be dropped because he couldn't follow the script. He carries the flight checklist, printed on a piece of cardboard, in the back pocket of his jeans. He has brought Jack and Anik Pendraud with him, breaking an unbroken rule of his own. Never, ever, involve yourself with clients on your own time. For one hour he could fly above the grass airfield in Alpha Whisky Alpha, a DeHavilland Tiger Moth, the last serviceable one in the district, and every second Saturday is his own time.

On his first joy-ride, at fifteen, Alec marvelled at the flimsy canvas and wire-strutted Moth, its two wings laced together with wire, as if to stop them flapping. Across his skull, the snug feeling of the leather helmet would cling and press into his scalp long after it was removed. *The Phantom, O Ghost Who Walks, O Biggles – O Red Baron:* the goggles, and the hug across a beating heart of the webbed safety harness. But most of all the open cockpit, where the joy-rider sat in the front seat, and he could pretend that it was he who was the pilot. And the wind, and howl of the engine, and the tower calling through the helmet headphones: 'Alpha Whisky Alpha, clear for take-off, runway zero-niner-zero.'

Jack watches Alec drain a cupful of fuel from the tank into an old Coke bottle and hold it up to the light. Alec explains to Jack the old-fashioned fuel check. They walk around the plane, feeling the fabric and checking that the wings and tail aren't about to fall off. Alec is aware of Jack's mixture of excitement and fear. Once he had read somewhere that real adventure comes always with a note of fear, including a paragraph of doubt and a sentence of regret.

Alec shows Jack how to climb into the front cockpit and secure the hatches and safety harness. He pulls the soft leather helmet over Jack's head and plugs in the radio lead.

'I can speak to you,' he tells Jack, 'through my microphone and the speaker in your helmet, but you won't be able to talk to me, okay?'

Alec waves to old Hawkins, waiting at the door of the aero-club, to come and swing the propeller and kick the engine into life. Hawkins has a hump between his shoulders and limps, and is known as 'Egor' in the club, where legend has it he turned his back on a prop — and it buried itself deep into the meat and bone of his back and left him with a lump the size of a monkey's head. Hawkins is not keen to flick propellers for Saturday fliers like Alec. He prefers the instructors with their student pilots who see him as a weathered old war man, full of stories and glories and horrors of the air. Alec knows that Hawkins has never been in a plane and never will be.

He reads from his checklist, as Hawkins counterwinds the propeller to draw fuel, and watches him kick the wheel chocks hard into the tyres.

'Fuel on.'

'Fuel on.'

'Contact.'

'Contact.'

The exhaust puffs blue smoke from under the cowling and

coughs. Hawkins's hump twitches in annoyance.

'Switches off.'

'Switches off.'

He rewinds.

'Switches on.'

'Switches on.'

'Contact.'

'Contact.'

More blue smoke, and the engine roars. Alec eases the throttle in, the sound becoming a chorus to conduct. He flicks the radio switch to intercom, and speaks into the microphone.

'You okay, Jack? Nod your head.'

Jack's black skull head goes back and forth. Hawkins removes the wheel chocks and limps back to the clubhouse.

'The engine has to run for a few minutes, then we'll take off,' Alec says into the microphone. Jack's head nods again. Alec turns the radio switch to 'Tower' and requests clearance for take-off.

Across the grass with the throttle full out — tail lifting the plane parallel to the ground, the stalks of paspalum bending in respect. And just before take-off: the fear, the doubt, the regret.

Imagined flight: unstuck from the ground — a breaking of the rules that have bound men forever and ever past to the earth.

And into the air: impossible. The dreams of ten thousand thousand men before, to swoop and soar and dip and glide.

Alec re-trims the flaps and climbs the plane to 3,000 feet. Beneath them the town of Camden stretches across the hills, its rooftops and roads placed by a giant toymaker, absorbed in his work. Directly underneath is the town cemetery which Alec uses as a marker to bank starboard and turn towards Burragorang Valley. He sees Jack's head tilt over the side watching the toy town as the plane leans into the air.

'What do you think?' he asks Jack through the radio.

Jack waves both hands above his head, shaking his fingers. Alec is not sure what he means.

'You okay?' he asks. 'Pat the top of your head if you're okay.'

Jack's hands bounce up and down on his helmet. Alec smiles.

Warragamba Dam has caused the valley to fill with water which sits, bottomless blue, in a vast basin of eucalypts: God's view — and Alec's and Jack's.

Alec remembers how Anik talked in the car about writers and books he had never heard of. Sometimes he bluffed about having read some of them and hoped she wouldn't ask his opinion. He was not accustomed to her way of discussion — he put it down to her 'foreignness'. Later, when she offered to lend him the books he was bluffing about, he laughed and asked, 'Did you see through me straight away?' 'One can always see one's own faults in others,' she had said.

They are directly over the water, and Alec pushes the joy-stick forward to get closer. As the plane noses downward, he is tilted forward in the cockpit and for moments there is the feeling of falling off a ledge; weightlessness with nothing to intervene. On the ground below, small farms had cleared the land into green and brown rectangles, and only higher up on the edge of the mountains, where machines couldn't chew, were the trees left alone. The valley, shown as a vast, neat cradle, seemed under attack. Alec banks the plane to begin returning to the airfield.

As the plane levels off, he notices how Jack's head is higher in the front cockpit than it ought to be. Jack's shoulders emerge above the plane's fuselage. There is no safety harness across his shoulders. Alec snatches at the microphone.

'Jack, sit down. Do you hear me. Sit down! You can easily be blown out. Put your safety harness back on. Jack, pat your head if you can hear me.'

Alec stares in horror as Jack rises even further out of his seat.

'Jack, sit down!' Alec is shouting into the intercom. 'Do what I say. Sit down. Put the harness back on. Jack! Jack!'

Alec eases the throttle inward to lose airspeed. Jack is kneeling on the seat of his cockpit. The cord connecting his helmet to the intercom prevents him from rising further. Alec cannot reach him.

'Jack, sit down!'

Alec bangs his open hand on the fabric of the plane, as close to Jack as he can reach. He sees Jack unclipping the chin strap of the helmet and then pulling it off his head. Alec watches it happening in slow motion. He shouts into the wind at Jack. And then Jack is standing on the seat. Alec heads the plane directly back to the airfield, his eyes fixed on Jack who is beginning to raise his arms outwards like wings. Alec has never felt so much fear in one moment in his life. Jack tilts his arms up and then down in imitation of aeroplane wings, then leans his legs into the back of his seat. The slipstream is yanking his hair backwards and his jacket is blown straight out and is flapping towards Alec's face. Alec considers grabbing hold of the jacket but envisages Jack's arms sliding out and him free-falling away. The thought makes his stomach heave and his hands go limp. He wills Jack to be glued to his seat.

'Sit down. Jesus Christ. Sit down.'

The airfield comes into sight. Alec wants to throttle on, but doesn't dare lurch the plane forward. The Tiger Moth has been losing height steadily at the low airspeed and Alec can see that they may not clear the trees along the river just before the landing strip. The radio is still switched to intercom, cutting out communication from the tower. Alec flicks the switch and immediately hears the tower call.

'Alpha Whisky Alpha, you are not clear for landing — go around. Alpha Whisky Alpha. Do you read? Alpha Whisky Alpha, you are not clear for landing, Alpha Whisky Alpha, acknowledge . . .'

Alec flicks the switch off and looks above and below for gliders. There is one several hundred feet above and to starboard. He cannot concentrate to call the tower for landing clearance. Up ahead, the trees seem like a giant hedge. He knows he will have to increase airspeed. With his left hand he gently draws out the throttle. The plane seems to float as if pulled by an invisible string down the hypotenuse of a triangle formed by ground, trees and flight path. Alec wants to shut his eyes. The trees look soft and cloud-like up close. Jack's coat is flapping in front of his face like a sheet on a Hill's Hoist.

And then it happens. Jack's coat rises up with his arms and falls away past the plane, like a gull at the beach. The plane clears the trees and lines up with the runway. Alec stares into the empty space where Jack stood. He cuts the throttle and pulls back on the stick, waiting for the familiar stall and flop onto the ground. There is nothing in his thoughts at the moment but the automatic responses of landing a Tiger Moth on a grass airstrip, and the emptiness of the front cockpit.

The landing is bad, and Alec feels the jolt through to his teeth as the plane stalls from too far off the ground, the tail skid scarring through the paspalum. His feet press hard to balance the rudder pedals.

And then there is Jack's head. Leaning over the side of the cockpit, staring face-on at the ground.

Alec cuts the engine as the Tiger Moth reaches the tar apron near its hangar. He has a sharp pain directly beneath his ribs, and his jeans, protected from the wind, are sodden with sweat. He removes his helmet, while his eyes are constantly focused on Jack. He steps into the foothole of the fuselage and reaches over to the front cockpit, grabs a handful of Jack's shirt-front and lifts him bodily from the plane.

Face to face with Jack on the ground, Alec feels a surge of anger and a desire to hurt Jack. For a moment he stands clutching Jack's shirt, his eyes screwed tight, his heart beating viciously. The sweat begins to cool on his jeans.

'Why did you do that?' He shakes Jack's shirt-front and Jack's body is thrown backwards and forwards. A button pops off and bounces across the tar. Jack watches it.

'Look at me, you little bastard. What the hell were you doing? You trying to scare me? Do you want to die? Is that it, you little bastard?' Alec lets go the shirt.

'I'm sorry, Alec.'

'Stuff your sorry.'

'I didn't mean it.'

'You could have been killed.'

'I'm sorry.'

'I could lose my bloody licence.'

'I'm sorry.'

Alec shakes his head and looks again at the plane.

'Sorry is always too late.'

His hands are still shaking as he squeezes them into a fist and out again. In and out.

'What the hell were you doing up there?'
'It was the wind, I didn't mean it.'
'Mean what?'
'To scare you.'
'It's no good, Jack.'
'It was the wind.'
'That doesn't make it okay.'
'I didn't think it was dangerous.'
'You're a liar.'
'I couldn't help it.'
'It's not okay, Jack.'
'Are you going to tell mum?'
'I don't know.'
'Don't tell her, Alec, please.'
'Don't tell her what?'
'What I did.'
'What did you do, Jack?'
'You know . . .'
'No, tell me.'
'You know . . . in the . . . plane . . .'
'What did you do?'
'You know, what made you scared . . .'
'Which was . . . ?'
'Me standing up.'
'And why was I scared?'
'I dunno.'
'Why was I scared?'
'Because I might fall out.'
'You knew that, didn't you?'

Jack doesn't move. He stares at the button ripped off his shirt, which sits like a tiny white wheel against a sea of black tar.

Alec can see Anik approaching. She wears red-framed sunglasses which reflect the light. He knows he must go to the tower and complete an incident report form. He will tell them that the radio cut out — a battery connection loose or something. His anger eases, draining inward. He looks down the field for Jack's coat.

The windsock, like a widow's hope-fooled wave to her husband's face in a crowd, rises on the breeze, sighs, and sinks.

Understand innocence, and that
all actions are forgivable.
Children and fools are not
innocent; they are unknowing.
To be innocent, one must know
of the trespasses possible.
So that he who is not capable
of evil, is not capable of good.

11

New Guinea 1967

Suli's father and Mennen's father have made and tied the burial platforms. They have left the three of us to paint the sharpened corner stakes and to weave the cover over the wrapped bodies of my father and mother. I tell them both to go for I wish to do this by myself. I have collected bowls of red and brown clay from the river and a white one I have made by crushing cave stone.

On my father's bed I will not paint the patterns of our line, for my father was a man not of his line but of himself. His thoughts were shaped by himself, alone. I will paint his story onto the platform and it will tell of a man whose strength was inside, whose knowing of things was made like carved neck beads, slowly and patiently. I will paint that he was not the father I wanted — that he was much more.

High up on the valley wall, I walk through the old gardens. There is no one here to take me outside myself. I tread slowly, as if the ghosts of those who dug the gardens sleep in the old mounds of earth. I know that the meris who scraped and planted in the mounds with their bilams bouncing against their backs and their babies seated across their shoulders would all be dead now.

I squat amongst the weeds and feel the roundness of the earth they dug so many times, so long ago. I feel their presence like wind on the top of the mountain.

'Where have you gone?' I want to ask them.

My father had said to me that at death, we are born into our dream of ourselves. I know my father's dream was to have the strength to stand against the weight of the line — to be free within himself.

Perhaps I am my father's dream.

Through the ancient gardens comes the sound of singing. It is a meri's voice and it floats on the breeze in pieces from high up the valley wall. I rise and follow the sound. It is a song that is sung at the tanim-heads and tanim-legs, in the haus-kundu. A song of flirting and touching between the unmarried meris and young men.

The singer is Gabi, the newly married woman from Tambul. She is surprised to see anyone in this empty place, but she remembers my face and smiles at me. She sits on a fallen tree. I see that she is thinner except for her belly, and she tells me there is a picanini inside. She has some taro and cabbage leaves which she shares with me.

I tell her about my father and mother and I ask her why she is alone, singing in this place. She tells me that her husband does not come to her now that she has the picanini and that she is alone with only his mother each day in the gardens. She wants to go back to her line, but they will not take her back as the marriage price was high and they could not return it to her husband's family.

'I could give you my father's pigs,' I say to her.

'A meri cannot give pigs.' She shakes her head at me.

'There are no brothers of my father, or mother — there is no one to have them.'

'The Tul-Tul would not allow it.'

'Then you are trapped.'

Gabi begins singing another song. It is an old song about a muruk who sees the beautiful feathers of his own body on the shining water of the river and becomes so jealous of the handsome bird that he smashes his claws and beak into the surface of the water to destroy the beauty of the other bird. But with all his fury, when the ripples fade, the beautiful bird remains. He comes to the river every day for his tormented fight. One day some small boys wait by the river and catch the muruk at the water's edge by his wing feathers which are torn out from his body as he escapes. When he returns to the river he becomes very happy, for the bird in the water is ugly and deformed.

I listen to the words of the song and watch Gabi rock backwards and forwards with the timing of the sounds. Her rounded belly has stretched the skin tight like a too-fat child. I think of the picanini inside, buried under the skin, and I reach out my hand and stroke the round flesh as she sings.

Perhaps the picanini will escape for Gabi.

12

Australia 1963

After dinner, Jack is in bed and Alec sits with Anik in the lounge room.

'Do you miss your husband — not living with you, I mean?' Alec asks.

Anik breathes in deeply and out through her nostrils noisily. 'Yes, in some ways, and in others, no. I know that for Jacques it's not good.' She pauses momentarily and then turns quickly to face Alec, grabs his arm with desperately dramatic passion. 'And the sex,' she says, narrowing her eyes. Alec is put off balance by the sudden shift in mood. Anik laughs. 'I could be an actress, don't you think?'

Alec regains his balance and laughs.

'I will make some coffee,' she says. Alec follows her to the kitchen, leans against the bench and watches her movements with the mugs and coffee.

'It is good of you, Alec, to make so much time for Jacques, especially his flight in the plane.'

'Wait till you get the bill.'

She laughs again. Alec marvels at the freedom of such a laugh and wonders why his own is always muffled or controlled in some way.

'Don't laugh,' he continues. 'The first time I paid for an hour's flying, the bill was so big I thought I got to keep the plane.' Anik laughs. 'They stopped me just as I was trying to tie it to my towbar.'

'You had the Tiger by the tail,' Anik quips back. Alec laughs.

Alec sinks into the lounge and blows across the surface of the strong black coffee. Anik lifts the lid of a woodgrained radiogram and places a record on the turntable. She returns to sit alongside Alec.

'This is Erik Satie, do you know him?'

'Not personally.'

'He was a cafe pianist in Paris before the First World War, before he became a composer.'

'Well, that explains it.'

'What?'

'I wasn't in Paris in 1913.'

Anik laughs. Alec notices the half-tumbler of whisky she holds in her left hand.

'Would you like something stronger?' she asks, holding her glass towards him.

'Coffee's fine.'

'I enjoyed our drive in the country — to your airfield.'

'I went to school out there — walked across that long wooden bridge twice a day for a lot of years.'

'It is a beautiful area.'

Erik Satie's piano notes fall cleanly in the air.

'Do you remember seeing those long vegetable gardens as we drove over the bridge? They belong to a family of Chinese market gardeners. They've farmed along the river flats for as long as I can remember — perfect rows of cabbages and carrots and beans. On the way to school, I used to shut one eye as I walked past and sight the other one like a gun barrel along the rows of vegetables. I used to watch them digging and picking, stooped over the ground. Half a lifetime of bending to the earth had them bowed like snagged fishing rods. I used to think that someone should do something about it — their shape, I mean — help them somehow. You know, put a knee in the small of their backs, pull on the shoulders and get their bodies perpendicular again, where they were supposed to be. I even had the idea that they could be staked straight, like their tomato plants. A good strong pole strapped down the spine, make it stay in its proper place. Of course they would never have been able to touch the ground again. I didn't realise that at the time.'

Alec focuses through his coffee mug as he talks.

'When I think of those times, I am always riding a bike through the bush with the sun on my back, and stuffed in my pocket, or tied to the bike, is some piece of junk I found at the local rubbish tip, which was going to astound everyone at home, and which I would make into something absolutely incredible.'

'And did you?'

'What?'

'Make something absolutely incredible?'

'No.'

Anik laughs along with Alec.

Alec considers telling her that she drinks too much. Is it any of his business? Would she say that to him? 'It is not your business.' If she asks would he like to kiss her? Alec looks at her mouth. She is drinking too much. Her mouth is opening and closing rapidly. She is talking to him and he has not been listening. He would like very much to kiss her.

'I think it was very different for me,' Anik says, staring past his shoulder. 'We moved to Compiegne, not far from Paris, when I was very young. We lived in the oldest house in town. Henry IV would meet his mistress in our house, Gabrielle d'Estrees.'

'Not while you were there, I hope.'

'I shall ignore your humour. The house had three floors, and my sister and I had one room called 'Chez Alice'. We would pretend it was like Alice's looking-glass room, and we would make up adventures, like Alice. We did it even when we were too old to do such things. I think my father would listen to us at the door sometimes, because at the dinner table he would ask us where we had been, and he knew we had not been out of the house. He taught me the poem at the end of *Through The Looking Glass*. His English was perfect, but now I can only remember part of it —

Still she haunts me, phantomwise,
Alice moving under skies
Never seen by waking eyes.

There is more but I cannot remember.'

'You miss your father?'

'We were surrounded by beautiful forests of beech and oak — I miss the forests, the trees here are different . . . harder.'

'And uglier?'

'Everything is softer there — the gardens, the rain, the light — even the people. They are not the same here. Here you are like gum trees, always defending against something; the elements, foreigners like me, and of course, each other. You are like Ned Kelly with his suit of iron.'

'Well, the French have Napoleon, the English have Sir Galahad, and we have Ned.'

Anik laughs.

'We all want to be bushrangers.' Alec feels the surge of excitement which comes when he makes someone laugh. 'You think I'm joking. A friend of the gang turned him in to the police — at a pub, would you believe, very symbolic.' Anik laughs.

'And the townspeople watched him being surrounded, their hero, and then shot.'

'It is so sad.'

'Ned wasn't too happy.'

'It is sad . . .'

'The idea is, that I only look short if someone else is trying to stand on a box, or wear a big hat.'

'I don't believe you.'

Alec knows it is true. Generations of arms bred for *pulling:* pulling hats over sunburnt heads, pulling the wool over someone's eyes, pulling the rug from under, pulling the plug on anyone who dared to float upwards. It was so difficult, the lifting muscles so weak, to lift anyone anymore.

Anik has moved closer, the right side of her body gently touches Alec's left side. She holds her mug in both hands and brings her head down to sip from it. He watches her. She smiles over the rim at him, listening to the piano music.

'I should like to play this one — it is called *Trois Gymnopédies* — when we make love.'

In surprise, Alec swallows too large a mouthful of the hot black coffee. It brings tears to his eyes as it burns its way down his throat and chest. With great control he maintains his relaxed appearance. He is not sure whether she said, or meant to say, that she likes to play this music when *she* makes love or when *we* make love — him and her. He watches her moving slightly out of time to the music, and begins to know that he would like to make love with her — with or without Erik Satie's piano notes.

'Did you know that Jacques writes little stories?' she says.

'Yes, he told me.'

'He told you?'

'Yes, I think it came out before he realised it.'

'He has not shown them to me — to anyone. I found them accidentally.'

'I can understand that.'

'That he hides them?'

'If he shows them to anyone, they may be lost to him — like telling a secret.'

'But why would he write if it is not to show anyone?'

'Perhaps having no secret is even worse.'

Alec would like to have words for his own secrets, and to tell them to someone, perhaps this strange woman. He would like to tell her about his fear that like Ned, there will gather about him a noisy, tearful crowd who will fall to their knees, open his vest, and find nothing.

He watches her stir more sugar into her coffee. The chiming sound circles inside the cup — the clatter of the silver spoon — a sound of chipping metal:

I'm Ned Kelly
with a cast-iron
belly.

13

New Guinea 1967

The Tul-Tul sits facing me on the other side of the fire. The house is different without my father and mother; it is older and lets more cold air through the walls. The Tul-Tul has said nice things about my father and mother, and I have thanked him. He has been to see the platform but does not talk of its wild paintings.

'Kaio tells that you go with Suli to the mission school,' he says to me.

I do not answer but look at the Tul-Tul's eyes.

'. . . and that you wear mission clothes. Is it true?'

'Yes. I am the only meri in the school room, and I learn quickly the talk of the Europeans. My father was pleased for me to go.'

'It is not for a meri to learn such things.'

'It is a white meri who teaches us.'

'The white misus is not the same — she does not have to work in the gardens and feed her husband's pigs and grow children.'

For a time there is a silence between us as the sounds of the fire can be heard through the house. Many thoughts rush through my head.

'What you say it true, Tul-Tul.' I watch the body of the Tul-Tul become calmer as the tightness leaves him. 'It is true what you say, I shall have to finish with the mission school to tend my father's pigs. There is no brother of my father's nor mine for them to belong to. And there are so many.'

'How many pigs does your father have?'

'He has forty pigs and five young ones. How many pigs do you have, Tul-Tul?'

The Tul-Tul sits back and looks at me with both shock and anger.

'It is not for you to ask,' he says.

'Now that I will not be going to school each day, I shall get them back from Mennen's father and look after them myself. My husband will be a rich man.'

The tightness has returned to the Tul-Tul's body as he sits taller and pushes wood to the centre of the fire.

'I will have to leave some pigs with Mennen's father in payment for his care while I have been at the school. My father would want the carer of his pigs to share his wealth.'

'You say that your father was pleased for you to go to the mission school?'

'Yes . . . he said that . . .'

'Then we must listen to his wish.'

'But the pigs, Tul-Tul, they cannot be left.'

'I have three wives who do nothing but fight and grumble, they should have more pigs to tend so that their days are not so empty. I will strengthen your father's wishes. You must go to the school as he wished, and I will tend your father's pigs.'

'The teacher from the mission has said that the Tul-Tul must be a strong man of his people to agree to a meri's going to school, and to stand against the words of others such as Kaio.'

'Hah, Kaio is a rubbish man.'

14

On our walk to school I tell Suli that I will punish Kaio for his trouble to me. Suli tells me that I should be grateful that the Tul-Tul allows me to go to school, and to forget about Kaio. I tell him about the Tul-Tul and my father's pigs. Suli says that my pigs will be very hard to separate from the Tul-Tul, but I do not care for I am still going to school.

'I will steal one of Kaio's pigs,' I say to Suli.

'And what would you do with it, you fool?' Suli asks with scorn.

'I will . . . kill it . . . and cook it . . . and eat it.'

'You are longlong, Kaio would crack your skull if he was to find you.'

'Hah, he would never find me.'

'You are longlong.'

'Will you help me?'

'No, I will not help you, you are a dangerous meri.'

'Did you hear that?'

'What?'

'Listen.'

'It is nothing, it is Sopol and the other boys, they wait along the track, in the bush sometimes, to tease me.'

'We will chase them away.'

'No, there are too many. It is a game, they mean nothing.'

'You are too weak for a man.'

'And you are too strong for a meri.'

'Am I?'

'Yes.'

'But I am good to look at — for a meri?'

'Huh!'

'You are not so good to look at for a man.'

'I will stuff your blouse in your mouth, meri.'

'Now you talk strong.'

Suli jumps onto my back, laughing, and I fall over with the weight, into the bushes, I fight him on the ground and soon I am on top of him with my hands holding his arms down. I am bigger than Suli and he squirms under me to be free. Suli stops laughing.

'Get off me, you witch, they will be watching — Sopol and the others.'

'Oh, but they mean nothing.' I copy Suli's voice.

'Get off me, or I will tear your blouse with my teeth.'

I can see three brown bodies in the distance, watching us. I get off Suli.

'I will let you get on top of me, if you like?' I tell him.

'Go away,' he says.

'So that they can see. Quickly, grab my arm and I will fall to the ground and sing out so that they can hear.'

'Be quiet, we will be late for school.'

We walk in silence along the track. The calls of the bush boys fade behind us.

'Why did you call me a witch?' I ask Suli.

'Because you are.' He turns around to face me and I see that there is hurt and anger on his face. 'Because many people say it; that you use the sorcery of the old people, sanguma; that your parents died on the same day; and that you go to a boy's school.'

'Who, who says this?'

'Everyone — and you won't go to your opening.'

'It is Kaio who says these things.'

'And others.'

'I will punish him, even without your help.'

'See, you talk like a witch.'

'Do you think I am a witch?'

'I am going to run now or we will be late.'

I run with Suli but inside, like seeds stamped into the mud, are the words: sanguma, sorcery, witch; sanguma, sorcery, witch.

15

Australia 1963

'You'll never guess what happened to me, Alec.'

'You've been arrested and charged with making obscene gestures in a public toilet.'

'They're sending me to Canberra for a public relations course.'

'The police?'

'The bank. They said I'm the first girl . . . woman in the bank to be sent.'

'Kate, that's terrific.'

'I was so excited, I rang mum up this morning.'

'They must think a lot of you.'

'I had no idea — Mr Gorman asked me to come to his office on the third floor, after morning tea, and he said I'd been chosen from fourteen applicants, and he asked me about you, and whether we had any plans.'

'What did you say?'

'I said, "No, not at the moment".'

'He wants to know whether you'll be getting married and impregnating yourself — and wasting their investment.'

'Do you think?'

'Maybe not.'

'It's very exciting.'

'I think we should celebrate.'

'God, I'll have to buy some new clothes.'

'Let's eat somewhere posh.'

'Canberra's a lot colder than here.'

'So is Antarctica.'

'I promised mum and dad I'd go around tonight.'

'Well, we'll go out another night.'

'Can I turn that music off? I'd like to listen to the news.'

'It's by Erik Satie, do you like it?'

'It's very nice. Last night they had aerial photos of missile bases they're building.'

'In Canberra?'

'In Cuba.'

'Erik Satie used to play the piano in coffee shops in Paris, before the First World War. Imagine old Erik plunking away in 1913 while everyone guzzled their coffee — and here we are, fifty years later, listening to the exact same plunks.'

16

'Tell me about your father, Jack. Why do you think he left home?'

'Are you here every day?'

'No, I have other schools I visit.'

'Which one do you like best?'

'Of the schools?'

'Yes.'

'Depends on a lot of things.'

'But which is your favourite?'

'I don't know, probably the high school at Camperdown.'

'Why do you like it best?'

'Oh, probably because of the variation — lots of different things happening all the time; bells ringing, phones ringing, necks that need wringing.'

'Are you going to stay doing your job?'

'I don't know. Tell me, when your father left, what happened at home?'

'Nothing.'

'Things went on just the same?'

'I don't suppose you'll take me up in the Tiger Moth, again?'

'Maybe.'

17

'I don't understand you, Alec.'

'Why do you need to?'

'I suppose for Kate's sake.'

'Your daughter is a big girl, Lorna, she can have her own understanding.'

'I can never tell what you might do next.'

'Makes me sound interesting.'

'It makes me anxious, frightened sometimes, and Kate too, I think. You can't predict what reaction you're going to have or what you are going to do or say.'

'You're making me anxious, Lorna.'

'Well then, why don't you . . . change.'

'How do I do that?'

'Grow up, Alec, you grow up.'

'I'm six feet tall, Lorna.'

'You know what I mean.'

'Be more serious?'

'You make it sound repulsive; that's another thing you do, you make other people feel . . . feel . . . sort of guilty.'

'Guilty?'

'For being sensible — it's true Alec, I'm sorry, Kate and I have talked about it before. You make people feel as though they are trivial or silly . . . I don't know what I mean, but it's something. You make people feel something — for being sensible.'

'And how do I grow up and out of this . . . this sillymaking?'

'I don't know, Alec . . . see, I'm feeling awful now, I feel like you are about to . . . make me feel like I'm wrong or stupid or something.'

'I can't make you feel anything.'

'But you do.'

'Well, that could be you making you feel it.'

'I don't know what you mean half the time . . . I might as well tell you all of it . . . I really don't know what you are talking about a lot of the time . . . like now. What do you mean *I* could be making me feel confused?'

18

'Alec, I think Jack Pendraud should go to a Special School.'

'I think he would be worse.'

'They know how to deal with boys like him — in smaller classes . . . there's something . . . something not quite *right* about that boy.'

'He's really getting a lot better.'

'He's not, you know, you're not the headmaster, you don't have to deal with him every day.'

'And you shouldn't have to either, Georgina should be able to cope with him.'

'I would like you to recommend that he be sent to a Special School.'

'I won't, Russell, he's better off here — even in Georgina's class; he has friends . . .'

'I believe you know his mother well?'

'Yes.'

'Perhaps that makes it difficult for you?'

'What do you mean?'

'Sometimes, when we get too involved . . .'

'I'm not too involved.'

'Well, then — do as I ask with Pendraud. I have the whole school to consider.'

'No.'

'You're backing me into a corner here, Alec.'

19

'Do you know, Kate, no one in your whole family ever touches anyone else — ever.'

'That doesn't mean anything.'

'I have never seen your mother or father kiss or hug either each other, or you, ever; not even when they haven't seen you for a while.'

'You don't see them all the time.'

'True.'

'Not everyone expresses affection in the same way, Alec.'

'I remember this American science film about an experiment with a baby monkey. They had a cell with two artificial mothers; one was made out of wire mesh and had a feeding bottle of milk that the baby monkey could drink from; the other one was made in the same shape but out of soft hairy cloth and bagging. When they let the baby live in the cell, the only time it spent with the wire mother was when it wanted a drink; the rest of the time it was cuddling up to the cloth one, even though it couldn't give any milk.'

'You just made that up.'

'No.'

'I'm affectionate to you.'

'I don't know that it's affection I'm talking about.'

'Alec, what is the point of this?'

'I don't know.'

'Do you want me to be more demonstrative, is that all?'

'I don't know; I wonder what you feel a lot of the time.'

'It's easy to be like that, Alec.'

'Like what?'

'Affectionate. I could easily pretend, if that's what you want, lots of women do, you know.'

'Pretend what?'

'Alec, what are you trying to get me to say?'

'I'm not sure, Kate.'

'I love you, isn't that enough?'

'What do you mean, "I love you"?'

'I think you're being silly.'

'Humour me.'

'. . . I don't know . . . I suppose it means we care about each other and we like the same things and we share experiences, and have the same . . . same . . . values . . .'

'You could be my best friend.'

'You are my best friend.'

'Is that all?'

'Alec, is this a cross-examination or are you devising some new theory?'

'Both; come here.'

'Not now, Alec, it's the middle of the afternoon.'

20

Anik tells Alec of her nightmare. Of how it is nearly always the same, except that each time a little more is added at the end.

I am in our bathroom at Compiegne, sitting on a wooden stool. I have no clothes on and my father is cutting my hair. His face is lathered for shaving with his razor. He hums a nursery rhyme to me as he snips at my hair. My back is itching where I cannot reach to scratch, and I cannot move my head. I can see myself in the mirror, framed by the doorway. My father smells of soap, and the hair of his armpit touches my face as he reaches upwards. Something happens, I do not know what; he begins to cut faster and to move differently. Hair falls into my face and into my eyes. It prickles and itches my skin. He becomes rougher and I want him to stop, it feels like he is cutting too much. He begins to sing a bawdy soldiers' song. My mother's face, only her face, appears in the mirror, sticking out sideways from the doorway. She has been watching. In two quick movements, my father swings the scissors down and snips off one of my nipples, and then the other. I don't feel any pain, and there is no blood. I sit and look at the flat, fleshy surface where the nipples were.

My mother comes into the room, smiling and making soothing noises and patting me. There is no hair left on my head. My mother puts her arm around me and takes me upstairs to my bedroom, where she puts me into bed.

In bed, I sit up and can see a perfectly blue sky through the window opposite. But it is raining. At the window, I see a face; it is Jacques, and he is looking at me, as the rain falls against the window. But it is not rain, it is not water, it is sand; and it piles up against the window, like the inside of an egg-timer. The itch that was on my back before is becoming very sore to touch and my hand can't quite reach it. It feels wet against the pillows. The sand outside is half-way up the glass, and Jacques kneels on top of it, staring into the room. I get out of bed and find a hand mirror and stand in front of the full-length mirror to see my back. At the window there is only a tiny line of blue above the sand. I am shaking with fear. There is sweat all over my body and I do not want to look into the mirror, and yet I want to look into it. In the mirror in my hand, I can see a large hole in my back, there is blood running down all the way past my spine and down my legs, and gobs and chunks of gore and split blood vessels and shining white bone hanging out of the hole. And at the edge, a grinning plastic soldier of Jacques's, chewing.

Alec does not want to explore what he knows to be images of a child abused.

21

New Guinea 1967

It is late in the afternoon, Suli has gone to his house and I wait in the bush near the garden of Kaio's sister. Kaio has taken a part of my freedom from me and replaced it with fear and now I will take from him.

Kaio has three pigs and two young ones, and they feed outside the fence of the garden. Kaio's sister watches them from time to time. I know that she will lead them back to her house soon and I wait for my chance. I have some warm kaukau in my hand which I spread on the ground near me. The smell brings the pigs who do not even notice me. I see a very young one who still drinks its mother's susu, and I lift it very gently so that it will not squeal. I tie its mouth with twine and place it in my bilam where its muffled cries cannot be heard over the noise of the others eating. I climb quickly up the mountain wall and off the track. The weight of the pig pulls me back and forces me to breathe harder. My heart is pounding for what I have done. I have never stolen before. As I claw at the mountain, it is as if Kaio and the others follow my trail. I stop and listen and there is no sound behind me. I go more carefully and do not break the ground or the branches of trees as I climb.

There is a small open patch of ground where I sit and take the young pig out of my bilam. It is even smaller than I first saw. I look at the ground and find a stone the size of my hand to crack its head. The twine has cut into its nose, and I untie it. The pig does not squeal, it pushes against my belly as if I am its mother. I hold its head still for the stone, but my arm will not swing. It is a stupid pig, for it does not know that it is about to die, that its movements now are of no importance. Its tiny legs tickle my belly. It is trying to reach my breasts, and I know that this pig has been fed by susu from a meri. I let it find my breast and feel its wet mouth on me.

It is a strange feeling which flows down through my body. I leave it sucking and pulling for susu that will not come. I wonder to myself if I am a witch, like Suli says. The young pig's body feels round and tight like Gabi's belly with the picanini. I hold its body against me. When it grows tired it stops pulling and folds its legs underneath itself and settles with soft, puffing breaths. I have some warm kaukau left which I offer to the pig, but it is too small to eat. I chew the kaukau in my mouth until it is soft and wet, and hold the pig's mouth open, spitting the kaukau to the back of its throat, as I have seen the old meris do with sick pigs. The young pig chokes and swallows, and waits for more.

I cut kunai to keep the pig warm and I leave it in a hole that has been washed in the ground from the time of the heavy rains. I will return to feed it in the morning. I feel sorry for the pig — that it is alone and that it is too late to return it to its mother, as Kaio's sister would have returned to her house and there would be an angry search for the lost pig.

It is becoming dark and I do not wish to be so far up the mountain as night comes down. I remember the stories of my mother, of Kuipa, the collector, and I race down the mountain with my feet slipping on rocks and my legs and arms scraping against unseen branches.

22

Australia 1964

As Alec pours milk into his mug of tea, a fifth-grade boy bursts into the staffroom, panting and looking from teacher to teacher, not sure which one to address or who is in control.

'There's a fight, sir, in the playground,' he puffs.

'Listen, son,' a male teacher swings around in his chair to face the boy. 'There's a teacher on duty out there, go and tell whoever it is, all right?'

'I couldn't find the teacher on duty, sir.'

'I'll go.' Alec turns the boy around by his shoulder. 'Lead on.'

'It's Pendraud, sir, and he's getting bashed up.'

Alec made a mental note of his increased concern. 'Jesus, is this my fault?' he thinks. For a brief flash, he has a picture of teachers murmuring how that Pendraud kid got a lot worse after the counsellor saw him.

In the playground, Alec sees a crowd of children squashing together and stamping in the dust, the mass swaying inwards and outwards like dog-rounded sheep. They jostle and scramble for a better view of the centre. A hundred shrilling throats crack like stock whips, blurring the air.

Alec is familiar with the excitement. The seduction of violence and fury released: terror and destructiveness, fuming impatiently below, looking for a cathartic moment, an excuse to ignite itself and breathe flame. Alec knows the dragon, how it is bred and fed and released. He has felt the shingles of its spine within himself.

The throng unknots in front of him with automatic respect. In the dust in the centre of the ring, Jack and Ian Isaacs are locked together, twisting and wrestling. For a fraction of a moment, Alec wants to watch, like the others, and then his school role descends like a blind on a night window.

'Get up!' he shouts.

The two boys roll over in the dirt. Ian Isaacs's right hand swings relentlessly into Jack's face. Jack's legs flail the air, attempting to encircle Isaacs's waist in a scissor lock. They roll onto the path. Alec hears the crunch of elbow and knee bones striking the concrete. A small trail of blood and skin is wiped across the surface. The crowd moves with the pair.

'Get up,' Alec shouts again.

The boys do not hear amidst the chorus. Alec grabs them both by the hair on top of their heads and pulls them apart.

'Enough!'

He turns to the crowd, which responds to his eye contact by closing its collective mouth. Consciousness ripples outwards from the inner circle. Some shorter boys at the back cannot see what has happened but automatically take their cue from everyone else, and settle into schoolboy silence.

'Go away,' Alec says to them with appropriate disgust. 'Go away, you'll all get your turn.'

The children dissolve into the playground, babbling and pointing back at Jack, each one imagining himself the winner, the maker of the pain; none of them sees himself as Jack.

Alec sends Isaacs to the toilet block to wash himself. Jack's face looks as though it has been dragged across the asphalt of the playground and ground into the dirt. The bony parts are wet patches of red and torn skin.

'I was just getting him then,' he says, hostile to Alec. His lungs heave and his whole body is shaking. 'I just got him in a scissors with my legs.'

Alec brushes at the dirt with his hands and then decides it is a waste of time.

'Do you hurt anywhere besides your face?'

Jack watches Ian Isaacs disappear into the boys' toilets. 'I'm not scared of him. I could have got him, I could have beaten him.' He gulps in air, and the words rattle with the effort to get out.

'Yeah, you were wearing him out all right.' Alec sees in Jack's face that it isn't a time to joke. 'Get your bag, I'll take you home.'

Alec tells the school secretary to inform the headmaster, the class teacher and to phone Mrs. Pendraud that he is taking Jack home.

In the car, Jack sits with his school bag on his knees, staring ahead. Alec drives slowly and takes the quietest road towards the Pendrauds'.

'What started it?' Alec asks.

'Isaacs.'

'What did he do?'

'Nothing.'

'Yeah, that can start a fight.'

'You're always making a joke, aren't you?'

Alec is stung.

'Only during the week — I have weekends off.'

'See.'

'I'm sorry. Do you want to tell me what started the fight?'

'No.'

'Okay.'

'I could have got him.'

'Maybe.'

Jack sits in silence. Alec glances at him sideways from time to time. The sound of the car's engine fills the silence between them.

'He said something about my dad.'

'Isaacs?'

'He shouldn't have said it.'

'What did he say?'

'I hit him in the face with my bag.'

'That was pretty dumb — he's a big kid.'

'He shouldna said it.'

'Are you going to tell me what he said?'

'No.'

Alec remembers his own first fight — his own fault, and he lost to a smaller, more savage boy named Malcolm Rogers, who left him the bump on the bridge of his nose and a desire never to lose again. Without thinking, Alec puts his hand out and onto Jack's shoulder.

'He shouldna said that about my dad.'

And Jack begins to cry. Great swollen, hoarded tears that roll into the raw flesh and soak up the dust.

Alec stops the car under the shade of a gum tree. And Jack leans his head against the dashboard so the tears won't sting his scraped face, and cries: thick, racking sobs from deep within his chest and stomach; the sound of a lost and wounded animal.

And all the while the tears, falling and falling into the carpet at his feet.

Alec is powerless, sickened by a vast swirling nausea for Jack and himself and a thousand others. A foolish, helpless compassion, piercing, like slivers of ice, the pit of his stomach.

23

New Guinea 1967

Outside the haus-kundu, I can hear the excited whispers of groups of unmarried meris. They are like dry straw before the fire of the tanim-head. Many of them have not been close to a young man from another line, and they shiver with the fear and the hope of the night. Mennen holds my hand tightly. This will be her last tanim-head, for her man will pay for her soon and she will be gone to his line many days' walk away.

In the haus we sit with our backs to the wall and our legs outstretched in front. Between each meri is a young man. On one side of me is Sopol, from a line close to Tabunak, and on the other side is one I do not know. In the singing, Sopol's leg touches mine and I do not move my leg away. Two of the young men have drums and they mark the movement of our bodies forwards and backwards to the music. I like the steady rocking together; we are like the body of a large animal and our minds are as one. The songs tell of old sing-sings and great fighting in the valley in the beginning. The young man I do not know sings a story of the masalai. The masalai who lives in the swamp; he is a spirit who can make himself a man or a meri. He moves through the swamp like the water snake and looks for young meris who walk alone and he twists himself around their ankles and slowly curls his way up their legs. After this song, the group is quiet — even the drummers do not move, and then a meri giggles, and the whole haus shrieks with laughter.

The young men tell of their own lines and of their hunting and their kina. The meris listen and whisper to each other. I see Mennen rise and go outside with the young man I do not know. Sopol talks of his father's pigs and the size of his gardens. Sopol's father has two wives and his mother is the first and oldest one. I have heard it said that she strangled her own picanini to punish her husband for taking a new wife.

I do not like Sopol's thinking, but he has a strong body and much land and many meris try to sit near him at the tanimheads. He asks me why I go to the mission school and I ask him why he teases Suli. He becomes angry and does not talk to me for two more songs. He asks me to go outside with him to talk alone.

Outside, there is no wind; the moon is strong and makes Sopol's oiled body shimmer like polished kina. Away from the haus-kundu, we sit together on a large rock. Below us the valley sits in grey patches from the shine of the moon. Sopol asks me what it is that I learn at the mission school. I tell him about the writing of words and the reading of them — about other lands which have black people and of giant villages built into the sky, and machines that can carry a hundred men. I tell him I have seen the pictures.

He asks me where all of the cargo comes from, and I do not know, but in time I will learn it, and that is why I am at school. Sopol remains quiet, and we listen to the night sounds; the small animals that must feed at night, whose mother and father is the darkness. I tell Sopol that I am glad that I am a creature of the light, but he looks at me strangely, and I think that he does not understand.

He tells me that soon the kiap will come from the Government station and there will be a counting of the people for the kiap's books. I can remember the last counting, but I cannot remember the kiap, for I was too small. Sopol says there will be a big sing-sing and pig kill at the time of the kiap, for he has heard the talk. To myself, I think that I would like to have some English words to say to the kiap when he calls me to his table, but I do not think I would be so brave.

From the bushes, I can hear noises which are not those of the night animals, and I see that Sopol hears them also. Quietly, we follow the sounds through the darkness. Ahead of us in the bushes are two people, lying on the ground. It is a man on top of a meri. I see that the meri is Mennen and the man is the unknown one who sang the song of the masalai. I pull on Sopol's arm to go quietly back to the haus-kundu; I do not want to know if the young man is inside Mennen.

The singing has stopped at the haus-kundu and many of the meris have gone. Two young men have been waiting for Sopol to return, they wave at him when he appears and rush up to him, grinning and talking quickly. Sopol says loudly that he will go now with his friends, and that he hopes we can meet again at the next tanim-head and have our pleasure again. His two friends look at me quickly and drag Sopol off, laughing like small dogs around their master.

The sting of Sopol's weakness slices like blade grass between us. He seeks to find, in the eyes and words of others, the image of himself. From my father I have learned that in pleasing others, the sight of ourselves can be lost; and I think that Sopol, in the search for his reflection, is already a blind man.

The others have gone and I wait for Mennen outside the haus-kundu. I think of before this night, and how Mennen and I made pictures of the promises it would hold; of the things that could excite and fly away with what we felt inside. And I begin to know that the hidden pictures in my head, like the moon-night shadows, can be stranger and more beautiful than the true shapes of the valley in all the light of the sun.

Each man is in a prison shaped
by his own hands, moulding clay
silted from a river of his
achievements. From the shallowest
turns of such a stream, the
strongest soil is scooped and
collected, without the least
ripple of danger.

24

Australia 1964

Alec is late for the staff meeting. The entire staff is seated in a horseshoe shape with the gap filled by the coffee-stained wooden table that protects the principal, deputy principal and infants' mistress. Alec finds a chair in the curve of the U, directly opposite the table. A few teachers smile encouragement at him. The deputy is talking about teaching programs and playground duty rosters. Alec scans the teachers seated on either side of him, their faces, expressions, positions. Did he ever feel part of this group? Was there any group he had ever belonged to? Alec was surprised by the thought: no, probably not. 'I am not one of these people,' he thinks, turning the thought over in his mind, examining it like a foreign coin in a handful of change.

And the whole room of teachers, synchronised: a Cyclopean eye is staring at him.

'Alec, are you with us?' The deputy is speaking to him and smiling patiently.

'I'm sorry, I wasn't listening.' A ripple of embarrassment rounds the horseshoe.

'About Jack Pendraud. Three complaints have been made about him this week. We were wondering if you had made any progress — anything to report?'

'No.'

'If anything, he's become worse.' Miss Benton's face is

flushed with her own daring. There are nods of support for her courage.

'That sometimes happens. He may get worse before he gets better.'

'That's not much help to us.' Miss Benton looks at the teachers sitting on each side of her. Alec watches her taste the thrill of group support, probably for the first time, and like coasting downhill without brakes, Alec pushes off.

'Frankly, Georgina, not much could help you.'

'Very funny, but you aren't teaching him.'

'Neither are you, Georgina.'

'There's no need for that kind of insult, Alec.' The deputy stretches his neck with anxiety.

'What kind of insult would you like?' Alec senses bodies stiffening, eyes to the floor — not to move, not to be picked.

'I think you should apologise to Miss Benton, Alec.' The deputy glances at the principal alongside him for approval and then stares at his notes in a manila folder on the table.

'I'm very sorry, for you, Miss Benton,' Alec says.

A group of male teachers try to laugh away their own fears, imagining themselves momentarily in Alec's place. The principal stands up and bangs the table with the palm of his hand.

'I will not have this kind of behaviour in my school,' he says, focusing into the distance over the heads of everyone seated.

'That's right, from now on,' Alec says, warming to the situation, 'there will be no behaviour in this school. Anyone found behaving will be tortured and burned at Friday's assembly.'

'I think you've said enough,' the headmaster says. Miss Benton can't resist a nip at Alec's heels.

'It's no wonder Jack Pendraud is worse after seeing you.'

'Everyone is worse after seeing you, Georgina.'

'I think you had better leave now, Alec.' The principal has taken off his glasses and uses his most serious voice. Miss Benton is close to tears.

'You think you're so smart, and you never do anyone any good,' she says, trying to rally support, as if something larger were at stake.

Alec's wit fails him, he looks at some of the satisfied faces in the horseshoe, and the ones turned away, and the few who are embarrassed. He walks to the door: *Straight rows; don't colour over the line; if we make an exception for you; sit up, hands up, shut up.*

'Get stuffed, all of you,' he says.

25

From his street window, Alec watches his parents get out of their car. His father leans backwards with thumbs pressing into his spine to relieve stiffness. His mother stretches into the back of the car and brings out a small wicker basket which Alec knows will contain vegetables grown in their back garden.

Not so long ago, Alec stopped being angry with them, which allowed him to recognise how he loved them both. It happened when he realised that they were more bowed than the Chinese gardeners by the weight of their lives: their afternoon naps and regular pills, and the endless ritual of meals which doled out the day like porridge into rigid bowls of time. Alec knew that traditions and habits were not always a sign of satisfaction; that a moth flaps and flaps, always in the same way, to get nearer the light globe that roasts its wings; and it is the rabbit who returns again and again to the safety of the same burrow who gets caught.

As his parents climb the stairs, Alec's last look at the street shows Anik and Jack parking directly behind his father's car. His heart lurches at the knock on the door.

'Hullo, darling — we've brought you some vegies from the garden, and your father needs to go to the toilet. There wasn't a public toilet the whole way.'

'Hullo, son.'

'I'll put them in the kitchen, Alec.'

Anxiety rises in Alec as he imagines Anik and Jack meeting his mother and father. Who is he concerned for? Anik? Jack? His father? Mother? Himself? He leaves the door open and notices his quickening breath.

Anik, holding Jack's hand, looks up to Alec from the stairway.

'Hello, Alec. I wanted to call in as we were going by. Jacques said there was some talk at the school — that you had some trouble with the headmaster?'

'My parents are here, come on in.'

'I'm sorry, Alec, we can come another time.'

'No, come and meet them.'

Jack is carrying his football and strides into the living room.

'Hullo there, young fellow.' Alec's father holds out his hands for a football pass. Jack smiles and tosses the football.

'This is Anik and Jack Pendraud — my mum and dad.'

'Hullo dear.'

'I'm sorry to interrupt you, but we were driving past and Jacques wanted . . .'

'You're not interrupting, dear — would you like a cup of coffee or tea — it's almost boiled, I'm making it anyway.'

'Rugby league, is it, Jack? You in the school team?' Alec's father squeezes the ball.

'I'm going to be.'

'I used to play real football, Australian rules, down on the border — in the ruck, I was. What position do you play?'

'Fullback.'

'Jacques was going to ask you, Alec, whether you would like to go with him to the football match on Sunday.'

'We used to play in bare feet.' Alec's father stares through the ball.

'I've got proper boots,' Jack says.

'Against the city boys, and the abos — and they had feet like tree stumps — ironbark tree stumps.'

Alec leaves Jack and Anik to be enthralled by his father as he goes to the kitchen and talks with his mother.

'Where's Kate?' his mother asks.

'Away on a course.'

'How is she?'

'She's fine.'

Alec watches his mother's hands moving amongst the cups and saucers like little animals: instinctive, knowing, repeating. The gold wedding ring almost invisible on the flesh-puffed fingers. Hands that had smacked him and stroked his forehead in hospital and rubbed Vick's Vaporub into his chest. Hands that had buttoned his shirts and wiped his face with a handkerchief with spit, and bathed his skinned knees in Solyptol. Hands that eventually waved goodbye to him and his brothers and sisters. Hands that brushed away a lifetime, like tears in the night.

'She seems very nice, this Mrs. . . . what's her name?'

'Anik Pendraud.'

'She's foreign, is she?'

'Swiss.'

'Does she have a husband?'

'Yes, they're separated.'

Alec watches the boiling water splash into the cups and listens to the underlife in his mother's messages.

'Older than you, is she?'

'Yes.'

'He seems like a nice little boy.'

'Jack?'

'Getting divorced, are they?'

'I don't know.'

'Have you know them long?'

'No, a few months. I see Jack at one of my primary schools.'

'He's a problem child, is he?'

'At school, yes. At home, he's fine.'

'Probably misses his father.'

Alec would like to ask his mother what he was like at eleven, but he has never spoken to her about such things.

'Do you remember Edith Hallet's little boy, Graham — when his father left home?'

'Yes, I remember.'

'Well, he went drinking a lot — so I was told, and he got mixed up with some big gamblers, and now he's disappeared without a trace.'

'I think Jack's off the bottle at the moment.'

'You can laugh, but I've seen a lot of these families. There's always something wrong with people who break up their marriages.'

Alec knows of the good intentions of his mother. She has been attempting to save him and his brothers and sister from disappointment, danger and disgrace all their lives. 'The three-D mother,' he used to joke with his sister. It was her way of loving. And yet she was enthralled by the risky success of others. Winning, to Emily Glover, was something designed for non-relatives.

'Alec, I found these brochures on your desk . . . ?'

'Uh huhh.'

'About becoming a cadet patrol officer.'

'Mmm.'

'In New Guinea.'

'Mmm.'

'You wouldn't do that, would you?'

'Probably not.'

From the living room, Alec can hear his father telling Anik and Jack about the 'old days'. When Alec was a boy, he wonders, did his father ever think that in those minutes — the minutes he was re-telling his endless childhood — were Alec's childhood and his future yarns?

Tom Glover remade his past over the years with spare bits of story like patched chicken-wire fence:

> The farm; the huge family; the shearing, droving and milking. And on horseback to school, where his legs were too long for the desk and his memory too short for the poems of damp English daffodils. Once, he and his brother stuck the wire handle of the kerosene feed tin to Daisy's horns in the milk shed, and she bellowed, trumpeting the noise back at herself from the tin. And she fled, straight through the wall of the shed, in terror, broken timber flying, leg rope dragging through the dust, until she hit the dam. Swimming and swimming in circles while the tin slowly filled with water, and Tom, dog-paddling out, couldn't get the wire over her horns. When Daisy couldn't

hear the bellowing anymore, Tom and his brother sat on the edge of the dam not knowing whether this was funny or tragic, but that they would get a belting when their father came home from town.

And sister Nancy discovered fainting. And the boys would encourage her on the way to school, so that all six of them had to bring her home instead of riding to school.

And the outdoor school toilet where Tom and Leo got a hand through the corrugated iron at the back, with a stinging nettle, and waited for Ivy Langendorf's little white bum. And watching all afternoon, with muffled hysterics, while she, the teacher's little dolly-pot, wriggled and scratched herself into legend.

And the cousin who dived into the creek and never came up — stuck under a log.

And the prickly pears that landed in the paddocks like spacemen that couldn't be killed.

And his mother's hair, black and shining as her fuel stove. Freshly washed, it unfolded down to the small of her back and coloured the whole of the room.

Underneath the laughter and the joking was the thread of mystery they all struggled with: their love and hate for a black man's country.

At sixteen, Tom found his mother dead. Leo and Tom and Nancy and Arthur and the others, each of them apart, stared at a land so dry that from their gut-spilled tears, not a single blade of grass would be born.

And Tom, the eldest boy, with so many mouths to feed, puts away his remaining childhood in his deepest pocket, alongside a keyring found in the bottom paddock, to be used if he ever has a key.

And later, working for money, bending to shear sheep all day so that it took two hours after sundown to straighten. Sitting alone with the other shearers on the back verandah of the boss's house, where the air carried fly spray and the swirling sounds of ballroom music from imagined dance halls five hundred miles away.

And Tom's young pony, Atlas, that wouldn't be caught. Round and round the paddock, and Tom's frustration and anger stacking and stacking like bales of hay in the sun. And when caught he cuts its throat with his pocket knife. Severing the only thing truly his — the only thing left to love. No more chance for pain. But the pain goes on; an ache in his chest, trapped for a lifetime, like stories, like his face in the mirror.

Alec would like to tell Anik that yarns can make a life truer than true — if they're told right and they're told enough.

26

New Guinea 1968

From inside my house I hear the feet of someone outside amongst the kunai. I cannot see into the darkness of the open doorway from where I lie. The fire has spent itself and sleeps in red coals under its ashes. I do not move and concentrate my ears on the feet outside. I wish now that I had listened to Suli and the others who tell me that a meri cannot live in a house alone. Near the fire, my hand finds my mother's pig stick. The feet outside move to the doorway. I cannot see and yet I know that someone stands there. I cannot speak, my voice is caught in the crashing between my ribs. I hear the feet enter the house and move towards the fire. I pull the pig stick to me and hold my breathing inside me.

I wait to strike at the shape that moves towards me. It is the shape of a meri with a large bilam. It is Gabi and my breathing comes out in a rush.

'Gabi!'

'Koam.'

Gabi swings her bilam to the ground and I sit up.

'Why are you here?' I ask. She leans her face forward into the fire and blows at the coals and ashes.

'Do you have wood?' she asks.

I place small branches with dried leaves across the coals as she blows, and watch as tiny flames and smoke arise. Gabi sits upright.

'I want to run away,' she says.

I look at her face in the light from the beginning flames; it has the tightness of hidden pain. I see that she wears all of the neckbands of her time before marriage so that her throat is completely covered.

'I will not go back,' she says to the flames.

I find some kaukau and place it on the edge of the fire and hand to her some pandanus nuts. We squat before the fire, cracking the shells with our teeth and watching the flames.

'You can live here with me,' I say. She looks at me and smiles.

'Two meris cannot live alone.'

'I live alone,' I tell her.

'But you are different.'

We chew the nuts, watching the flames and turning the kaukau from side to side.

'How am I different?' I ask. Gabi looks at me and then back at the fire.

'They say you are sanguma.'

'Who says this?'

'Many of the old meris.'

'Do you think it?'

'They say that your mother and father die on the same day and that it is sanguma, and that you will not set the time of your opening and that you go to the mission school, like a boy — and that you live alone and the masalai comes at night to you.'

'You are my only night visitor and you do not look like the masalai.'

Gabi looks with shock at me, and then sees my face and laughs. And I laugh with her.

'Perhaps you *are* the masalai,' I say, and we both laugh with loud noises until the tears run down our faces.

As the fire rises stronger, I can see her round belly above the cord of her laplap. I think of having a picanini growing in me and I wonder at two persons caught inside the same skin. I ask her what it is like to have this. She does not understand what I ask, and I do not know clearly myself. I ask about her husband and she says that she does not know him and he does not come to her since the picanini began.

I listen to Gabi talk, but in my head I see the baby pig I stole from Kaio, trapped in the dirt hole in the ground. I see it leaping up the walls and wearing tracks into the dirt and I see it falling back into the hole and giving up in the end and only waiting.

'Where will you go?' I ask Gabi. 'If your line will not have you.' She looks at me and her face is like the empty paper at the mission school.

For a long time we sit and watch the fire. Sometimes she sings softly and rocks on her heels. She tells me of her mother's house and of a time when she was punished for causing their house to burn to the ground. She was a small child and she had stacked branch after branch on the house fire to see the flames go higher and higher — until the roof joined in, and they were all of them almost burnt. She was beaten by her mother until the bones of her back had no skin and her mother could not raise the stick. And never again did she stoke a fire to the roof.

Through the doorway I see the sky becoming lighter. The weight of the night is being lifted by the sun. My eyes are thick with their need for sleep, but I sit with Gabi and listen to the humming sound of songs that have no words. I tell her that I must go to feed a young pig that I have hidden in the bush. I tell her of how the pig was stolen from Kaio and placed in the hole. She looks at me like the children look at the old men when they tell stories of the times before — of the killing times. She wishes to come with me and I know that it is both to see the captive pig and to not be alone.

It feels good to have someone with me. Along the track the small birds call warnings to each other and flap amongst the scrub. The ground is wet and squeezes cold mud between my toes. It is a long and steep climb, above the gardens and through the rocks and past the fallen trees. I tell Gabi why I have taken Kaio's pig but she does not say anything. When the track is wide enough for us to walk side by side, she holds my hand. Damp clouds of the day before still hang amongst the trees along the top of the mountain. The light still struggles to lift the darkness.

At the edge of the clearing, I stop and quiet Gabi with my hand held up. When there is no sound, I walk to the hole. At the bottom I see the small pig stand when it senses my movements. I lie on my stomach, reaching down into the hole and lift the excited pig by the front legs. It is hungry and dances around shaking and squealing. Gabi laughs as she watches. I chew the kaukau I have brought with me and feed it to the pig. It makes choking sounds as lumps of the food catch in its throat.

The mist is heavy this far up the mountain and the cold settles on us as we sit. The pig struggles to get closer to the warmth of my body and climbs onto my laplap. I warm its small body with my hands and it ceases to struggle. Gabi's hand touches my shoulder and I see that her eyes strain through the mist towards the edge of the clearing. She turns her head to hear what she cannot see. Her touch is cold, as if her hand has dipped chilled fingers of fear into my blood. I can see nothing in the direction she stares, nor can I hear movement or sound. I think of Kaio; of how he would have searched for his lost pig and how he could have found it in the hole and waited, waited for the thief to appear, waited for me. I cannot leave the pig in its hole again, I do not know why. I place it in my bilam, carefully and quietly. My legs want to run down the mountain and back to my house but I watch Gabi and her concentration on the same spot at the edge of the kunai.

I want to say to her that it may be Kaio, but I am afraid to speak. She stands, and I rise, holding her hand in mine. She whispers something that I cannot hear; her face is still turning away. And then we are running. Down the mountain. Crashing through the overhanging bush, our feet bruising the ground and flinging the mud up our legs. The body of the young pig bounces against my back, and sweat slides into the scratches and cuts made by the palm leaves. I think only of outrunning what is behind us. I see blood between my toes from stone cuts on the bottom of my feet but it does not slow my pace. It is as if I am falling from the face of the valley: a picanini tipped from her mother's bilam.

I do not know if I hear the sounds of our follower behind us but my chest hurts from the cold air that is fed too fast to it and the bilam strings cut into my head from the weight of the pig. I know that Kaio will kill me if he catches me.

We leap across the fallen trees and through the giant rocks that mark the end of the old gardens. I know that I cannot carry the weight of the pig and run so fast any longer — it weighs me down and slows my legs. I stop behind the largest rock and empty the pig onto the ground where it squeals and runs to snuffle at my feet. Behind me Gabi stops, her breath heated to steam from her mouth, speaks to me but I cannot hear clearly, the sounds are strangled in her chest and my thoughts are running ahead down the mountain. I look at the baby pig waiting for me to lift it up and into the warmth again. And it is then that I hear the words of Gabi.

'His feet . . . his feet,' she says.

I do not hear clearly, and I do not understand, for we are running again. For a little while the young pig runs with me, but it cannot keep up, and I will not slow my running. Through the rocks and onto the old tracks worn into the ground, where the water runs in tiny rivers and the grass never grows. My empty bilam, flapping without use, is cold where the pig's body was warm. At the top of the old gardens, I turn and in the distance there is the baby pig running, but it is on the wrong path and will never find me. I look for Gabi and she is not there.

27

Australia 1964

The back verandah of Anik's house is decorated with streamers and balloons. It is wide enough to easily fit an old wooden table which is covered with paper plates of potato chips, jelly beans, licorice allsorts, pieces of honeycomb and glasses of lime cordial. There are six party hats pointing their cones to the corrugated iron roof which stretches and ticks as the sun escapes seemingly motionless clouds. Alec likes the rambling nature of the house and the cool ease of the shade on the verandah.

Jack is eleven today, and Alec has been invited to his party along with David Johnston, Eric Millson, Mick Warwick and Stacka Van der Hoeven, all from Jack's class. Alec is surprised that Stacka has been invited — he is not usually wanted at parties. He is fat and slow-moving and wears odd-looking clothes. He speaks with a thick Dutch accent. The only fame he has found is in the playground where the game 'stacks on the mill' means Stacka Van der Hoeven is worth four others.

'Jacques made out the invitations,' Anik says as she tips salted peanuts onto a plate on the table. 'He said that if he doesn't fall on you, then Stacka is all right — and according to Jacques, he knows everything about the world.'

Alec looks at Stacka's present to Jack: a large book entitled *Wonders of the World*. David's present was a cricket ball wrapped in Christmas paper and Eric brought a neatly packaged matchbox car. Mick came with nothing. Alec watched him shake hands with Jack like an old man, and Jack made Mick feel better by reminding him that Mick gave him an ice-block two weeks ago.

Mick is small and quiet and seems to Alec to be someone who bridges all the sub-groups at school. Alec had seen him approached by other children to settle disputes and chaos in the playground. Eric is a follower of David Johnston, and puts up with off-hand treatment in order to be visible at all on the edge of the spotlight that regularly focuses on David. David is tall and bronze-coloured, with the languid, loping movements of a natural sportsman. He excels at anything physical, and even Alec is impressed at the ease with which new physical feats are absorbed by his body. David appears to contain no malice, violence, or need for power. Alec has thought that perhaps David has little interest in others, that his curiosity, challenge and need to understand focus entirely on his own body. He is impossible to dislike, but Alec thinks he may also be impossible to like. David's power grows as followers believe that his unconcern for others stems from strength, rather than emptiness.

The boys at the far end of the yard bowl the new cricket ball at a cardboard box propped against the fence. Anik sits alongside Alec on the verandah.

'Would you like to be that age, again?' she asks. Alec thinks for a minute as he watches the boys.

'No,' he says. Anik is surprised.

'Was your childhood unhappy?'

'I don't believe in going back.'

'I would go back.'

'And repeat everything?'

'No, I would go back wiser — with what I have learned.'

'Then you wouldn't see or discover the same things — it would all be different.'

'Perhaps you are right.'

'The past is beautiful because it is untouchable.'

Anik looks at Alec as the cricket ball is smacked by David Johnston against the fence.

'Do you think Jacques is happy, Alec?'

'Some of the time.'

'I cannot understand much of him now.'

'What do you mean?'

'He is becoming an Australian boy — and I am not.'

'You certainly are not an Australian boy.'

Anik laughs. 'You know what I mean.'

'I think so.'

'I would like to send Jacques to a boarding school, but he refuses to even discuss it.'

'His friends are here.'

'Yes, they are very important to him, I can see that. I think I have selfish reasons as well for Jacques to be away. I would like to be free again, like the boys.' She waves her hand at the boys playing cricket. 'Sometimes, I would like to deliver Jacques to my husband. Jacques idolises him, but I could never do it.'

'Why do you live apart?'

'That is a long and painful story, and one day, perhaps I will tell it to you.' Alec looks closely as she speaks.

'We must get the boys to play a proper game,' she says.

'A proper game?'

'One which has rules and turns — we shall play charades.'

'Charades?' Alec says as he watches the cardboard box disintegrating with each blast of the cricket ball.

Anik steps down from the verandah and claps her hands together to get the boys' attention.

'Boys, boys, come, we will play a game that is a lot of fun, come, come on Jacques.'

The boys look at Alec as if he should do something to save them. Alec covers his eyes with his hands and shakes his head in mock sympathy. The boys wait to follow Jack's lead. He approaches his mother cautiously.

'We will play charades,' she says with great excitement, clapping her hands and bouncing up and down on the balls of her feet. The boys look at Jack who looks at Alec. Alec offers no help. Jack looks at David Johnston who is expertly flicking the ball into the air and catching it at the last possible moment before it hits the ground. Mick picks up the cricket bat and walks over to Anik.

'Is that the game where you have to guess what people are doing and they can't say anything, Mrs. Pendraud?' Jack runs up to Mick.

'It's a great game, mum and dad and me play it all the time.'

'I've always wanted to play that,' Mick says. 'Since I saw it in a movie.'

The other boys follow Mick and Anik and Jack onto the concrete steps and drape themselves against its smooth coolness.

It is no surprise to the boys that Stacka is the best at charades, he seems to know the solution before the actor finishes. Anik's laughter and exuberance become infectious and the boys slap each other and squeal with delight and fall about on the steps and the grass. Alec enjoys the sounds which rise and fall like a frivolous melody.

After the game, the boys sit at the table with paper party hats held on with elastic that stretches under their chins and presses into the flesh. Anik and Alec bring plates loaded with steaming hot cocktail frankfurts and sausage rolls. There are toothpicks to spear the frankfurts and dip them into the tomato sauce.

At the end, there is the chocolate birthday cake with eleven candles — Jack has explained each detail of the ritual to Anik, and with Alec's guidance, she has got it right. Jack is happy and excited. He blows the candles out after making his wish. He is eleven and everyone claps for Jack. He catches his mother's eyes on him as the candles still smoke, and she says:

'Happy birthday, Jack,' — not Jacques.

It is almost dark, the food table has been cleared away and the seven of them sit along the verandah. The boys sprawl along the timber flooring like spilled marbles: and they talk.

Anik tells them what it would be like if they were French or Swiss boys. They listen closely. Stacka tells what his mother has told him of Holland. The strangeness of unseen worlds descends on their consciousness like night dew on grass, and they struggle to absorb it. Mick talks about his older brother who left to work on a merchant ship and who sends back postcards of exotic islands and picture-book cities full of mysterious people. David tells how he wants to go to England to play cricket for Australia, and Eric says there is an Italian migrant family next door to him and that Italy sounds pretty interesting but he doesn't think he would really like to go there because they don't speak Australian. Jack says his father is going to travel the whole world with him and they are going to buy a boat and sail everywhere and stop when they want, as long as they want, and they will take photographs of all the different people and they will help poor people and have friends in every country who will want them to stay, and on a boat everyone has to stay close together.

And thc talk goes on into rhe darkness which settles patiently around them, as if waiting and listening, waiting and listening: inhaling dreams.

28

On his way to the staffroom, Alec is told by the school secretary that the headmaster would like to see him. The secretary is a patient and gentle lady, close to sixty, and Alec is her favourite person in the school. He has listened to her talk about her husband's retirement and how it had changed him. Alec has brought her cups of coffee at times when it wasn't even her tea break, and he has sat on her desk and just listened. They have talked for embarrassingly long hours yet nobody has ever dared say a word. He is the only one who calls her by her favourite name, 'Maggie'. She believes Alec is unaware of his effect on most people; a disturbance of some kind, she feels, but lacks the exact words for it. Most of the teachers respect him, she knows, but she has watched their fear that he will not abide by the rules, that he will force something out of them — a reaction, a truth — when all the rules clearly say not to do that.

Maggie is concerned for him now because the headmaster has said enough to suggest that their meeting is going to be more than unpleasant.

'Alec, is everything all right?' she asks quietly.

'Fine, Maggie, and what about you?'

'Oh, I'm fine too.'

Alec walks off in the direction of the headmaster's office. He has always forced himself to get along adequately with Russell MacLachlan, despite differences in almost everything. He did seem to care about his staff and the students. He liked to transmit a fatherly image, needing the staff to come to him with their problems. Alec remembers how angry Russell became once when a teacher talked to Alec about her classroom and personal problems — and Alec refused to discuss it with him. A father, but a jealous one: love on conditions.

The headmaster shuts the door quietly as Alec sits down opposite his desk.

'Sit down, Alec — it's time we had a talk. I've been concerned about you lately.' He sits back in his chair with his arms folded acoss his chest. 'Now what seems to be your trouble?'

Alec feels like a child and suppresses a smile.

'I don't know, Russell.'

'We can't let you behave like that — like you did the other day at the staff meeting, not in front of the whole staff. It was most difficult for everyone. Now what's gone wrong?'

'I don't know.'

'How are things in your personal life, Alec?'

'Good, Russell.'

'That's good, Alec. What about here at school?'

'No.'

'Is there anything I can help you with?'

'No thank you, that's very kind.'

'My job is to look after my staff, Alec — after all, you all run the place, I just oil the cogs occasionally.'

Alec pictures the headmaster with a long-funnelled oil can, dosing the staff.

'Actually, you could do me a favour.'

'Yes?'

'Could you stop caning Jack Pendraud for a while?'

'Ah, now that's another matter.'

'You asked whether you could help — that would help, I don't think it's having a positive effect on the boy.'

'Well, Alec, you know I don't like giving pupils the cane. As a matter of fact, it's the last action in my arsenal that I like to take. But I *do* have to support my staff, and they must be able to count on that support, otherwise we'd have chaos in some of the classes.'

'You know Georgina is a hopeless teacher — any child with half a brain is going to be bored to insanity.'

'She's qualified and does her job, Alec.'

'She's an idiot who fills in the roll and arrives on time.'

'I can see we're not going to get anywhere with this. It's not your concern how she teaches.'

'It is if it causes half the problems I'm supposed to fix.'

'Well, you refuse to recommend the boy for placement in a special school . . .'

'He would get a lot worse there and you know it.'

'That's not necessarily true, Alec, but we would certainly benefit.'

'Georgina would have no one to blame.'

'I want you to take some leave-without-pay.'

'That's not going to make all that much difference.'

'Otherwise I will have to suspend you from duty, Alec.'

'Are you serious?'

'I have written approval from the district inspector. I have everything you've said recorded.'

'Suspended? I thought that was for pupils.'

'And staff when they act like children, Alec — and when they fail to do their duty properly.'

'And how would you know if I was doing my job properly?'

'Don't raise your voice at me.'

'Don't tell me you know anything about my job!'

'I'm the principal here!'

'And I'm the bloody counsellor.'

'I've taught more children in my career than you've read about in all your university books.'

'And you've learned nothing from them.'

'I taught!' The headmaster's face is flushed with red veins pumping, he gasps for air. 'I didn't have time to *learn*. But I'll tell you what I have learned. I've learned that smart-arse new teachers, with their psychology and philosophy, can't bloody well teach!'

'And dumb-arse boys who can't do any better become teachers who teach that six nines and the fucking capital of Iceland will get us all through life. And I'm not a fucking teacher — I'm a school counsellor.'

The headmaster's eyes narrow. 'And to this school you are useless!'

'And to this world you are harmful.'

'You're suspended, Alec.'

'And so are you, Russell — by invisible strings.'

'I'll send your letter of suspension in the mail.'

'Thank you.' Alec walks to the door and the headmaster shakes his head ruefully.

'You and your lot are always so clever, and sure of yourselves — so sure you're absolutely right.'

'No, Russell, only sure that you and your lot are absolutely wrong.'

'I've arranged for Jack Pendraud to go to a special school, without your recommendations.'

'Get stuffed, Russell.'

Maggie is visibly upset as Alec closes the headmaster's door. He realises she would have heard some of the shouting.

'Alec . . .'

'Yes, Maggie.'

'I'm sorry . . .'

Alec smiles and gives her a wink.

'Don't be sorry for me, Maggie.'

29

New Guinea 1968

To walk with Suli to the mission school each morning has become a secret pleasure; like watching the old meris pat the river clay over and over with flat sticks until, little by little, a shape emerges. Together we try new English words on each other, and the bush. Suli knows almost all of the English words and I know hardly enough to fill my mouth, but Misus Kane says that the words that I know are said well, and I am pleased. I have bought another blouse with my father's kina and I like its colours. They are brighter than the colours we take from the ground, but they do not stay in the blouse for long with washing in the river. Much of the cargo from the mission store disappears like chalk on the school board and leaves nothing of having been at all.

I wonder that the whites, with their cleverness, do not make things to last. Perhaps their cargo is as plentiful as our tanket leaves.

Suli talks to me about the minister who came to the school and spoke to us about giving ourselves to God. He was old, the minister, and tall, with red-coloured hair and a loud voice which made me wish that I had sat at the back of the class. Suli was captured by his words and sat in his seat after everyone had left.

'I will be a minister,' Suli says. I do not answer. There is nothing to say to one who has such a look in his eyes. 'You do not think that I could be one, do you?' he says to me. I walk in silence. 'I will be a minister — I shall wear long clothes and a white neck collar, and people will come to hear me talk.'

I see Suli in my mind in his minister's clothes, standing on a platform higher than the people he speaks to; he holds a large black bible in his hand and gazes up towards the sky.

'You could be a minister,' I tell him. He looks at me when I say this, to see if I am teasing him, and he is pleased when he sees I am not.

'There is another school, after this one, a bigger one, by the sea, if I want to be a minister.'

We walk on together thinking of the bigger school which lies somewhere along the lowlands near the sea.

'Can meris go to this school?' I ask him.

'You will not be concerned with another school.'

'Why do you say this?'

'Because Wahgi is going to buy you — my father told me.'

Suli's words do not surprise me. I have seen Wahgi look upon me for many months. His land, and the land of his line, lies next to my father's, and he has known me since I was a picanini. I remember before the sickness of my father and mother, seeing him standing above me in the gardens. He was dressed for the men's haus, and he stopped and stood tall against the garden fence watching me. I saw his wig stuffed with yellow swamp daisies and the brown and white earth striped carefully across the bridge of his nose and cheek bones, and the half-moon of the kina shell around his neck. And down his chest the longest pit-pit ladder, telling of his pigs and kina and wives. He saw that I was alone in the garden and he spoke to me — words that he would not have had others hear, and they have not left me.

'I have watched you,' he said, 'with your mother, and in play with the other children. You do not follow — you are a meri with much strength, and I will have you as my wife; I will give you pleasure at night and you will bend to me.' I did not run as my legs wanted, but stood and stared back at him. 'You do not run from me,' he laughed. 'You are like the pig that will not turn from the fresh garden. I will turn you, little Koam, like the wayward pig.' I had seen such pigs, the ones who would not trot along the path when the old women tapped at their snouts. They would break into the bush and head back for the fresh kaukau plots with dreams in their heads of unprotected mounds where they could root amongst the plants and toss soil into the air and dance free. Only pain would make such a pig give up its dream — and I have seen the men hold the pig between their legs and break its teeth with rocks, while the old women watched with approval.

Wahgi leaped over the garden fence and came close to me and still I did not move away, and he touched me and this, too, has not left me.

At night, by myself, I think of Suli going away to the bigger school by the sea. I know that I am not one of the mission people. I could not give myself to their God. I wonder if I am one of my own line.

I think of Wahgi wanting me and how my father would have been proud to sit down with him to listen and to bargain for me. To live alone, I must find people within myself; those that have put themselves there with love, and the night, then, does not weigh down so heavily it cannot be lifted.

30

Australia 1964

Alec follows Miles through the swinging doors of the Railway Hotel.

'How do they come up with the names, eh, Alec?' Miles shakes his head in awe. '"The Railway Hotel", how do they do it?'

'It must be a gift.' Alec joins in the joke.

'The Railway Hotel, makes you just shiver, doesn't it?'

'Or throw up.'

'Which enables you to drink more.'

The barmaid approaches and Miles grins at her. 'Two tickets to inebriation, please,' he quips.

'I like a man with a sense of humour.' The barmaid's face and mouth do not seem to move. 'My husband had a sense of humour — made jokes about sick people and then it happened to him.'

'What?' Miles is not sure whether he should be laughing or concerned. He looks to Alec for help.

'Dropped dead right where you're standing.'

'I'm sorry,' says Miles, souring his smile.

'I'm not — funniest thing he ever did. Now what'll you have?'

'Two middies of Resch's, please,' Alec says quietly.

'Only joking, boys. Name's Joycie,' she says as she moves up the bar to pull the beers. Miles's happy face returns.

'Nice lady,' he says.

At the other end of the bar there is an old man in a brown cardigan and an ancient, sweat-stained felt hat. The hat is pushed back off his forehead as he listens, expressionless, to the races. One elbow leans into the towelling spread along the bar to soak up the condensation. One hand holds his dripping glass of beer. His skin is a charred offering to a lifetime of outdoor work; brown splotches and flaking skin along the ridges of his cheekbones and nose: white man in a black man's country. Alec indicates with a movement of his head.

'I've seen him before.'

'Yeah?' says Miles.

'In every pub in Sydney.'

'Yeah?'

'You get one of him when you buy a hotel lease. He's the pub gnome.'

'He looks a sour little bugger.'

The pub gnome takes out cigarette papers and a tin of Champion Ready Rub tobacco and begins rolling his own cigarette.

In the corner, hovering over a pinball machine, are four young boys. One of them slams his palm down on top of the glass in frustration. The owner's head rises behind the bar. 'That'll be enough of that, young fella,' he says in his publican's non-offensive voice.

'What have you been up to lately?' Miles asks.

'Not much, what about you?'

'Same old routine.'

'How's Deirdre?'

'Old Deirdre? She's just the same. She wants to get engaged now.'

'Does she?'

'I suppose it's about time.'

'We'd better drink to that.'

'Yeh, it makes me thirsty talking about it. How's Kate?'

'She's in Canberra on a course.'

At the end of the bar, the gnome is joined by his mate, a soft-skinned, flush-faced man who has his own National transistor radio tuned to the races and held up to his ear. He sits down and Joycie automatically places a beer in front of him. He says something to his mate and they both concentrate on the radio. Miles orders two more beers. A group of Italian building workers comes through the door, all of them talking at once in their own language.

'How's the flying going?'

'Good, I was up last weekend.'

The noise in the bar increases. The gnome turns up the volume on his radio. Alec watches the Italians. Some of them wear blue singlets and two of them have handkerchiefs tied around their necks with a certain unselfconscious flair. No Australian would ever do that, Alec thinks.

'How's life at school?' Miles asks.

'A few problems at the moment.'

'Well, you can always have a job with me.'

'Fenton's Gymnasium Wonderland? I couldn't stand the boss.'

'Me? People queue up for the privilege.'

'To get their pay more likely.'

'Ha.'

The gnome pats his mate on the back. The mate, whose face is even more flushed with excitement, grabs his friend's hat, puts it, clown-like, on top of his larger head and twirls giddily around. The gnome gruffly snatches it back, with feigned impatience. He has obviously won on the last race. He gives Joycie a big tip and she says something flirtatious to them both. The clowning, soft-skinned one laughs, and slaps the gnome's back again. The gnome pretends he is annoyed. Alec guesses that both of them are married; their clothes are too well-ironed and chosen. He watches their ease together: men bred to flock safely with other men, trained by mothers to give sheepish smiles to female foxes — and never let them in.

Miles reads from a newspaper left behind on a stool. 'Martin Luther King, have you read this? Reckons he got a million blacks to march on Washington.'

Alec thinks of a million blacks all in line, marching towards Washington. Miles folds the paper and leaves it on the bar.

'Let's have another beer and go and do something ridiculous,' Miles suggests.

'We are doing something ridiculous.'

'That's true. No, I mean really ridiculous, that we've never done. Let's go to a house of ill-repute.'

'We *are* in a house of ill-repute, The Railway Hotel.'

Joycie looks over at Alec and raises one eyebrow, as if they have been naughty boys. Miles looks up.

'She has ears like a . . . like a . . . what has got big ears?' Miles asks, pretending to be more drunk than he is.

'An elephant.'

'. . . Like an elephant. No, an elephant has *memories*. She has ears like a fox — and big memories, too.'

'A fox has cunning.'

'They have big ears, too.'

'No, they don't. Four legs, one nose, and two cunnings.'

'That's only the females.'

Most of the Italian men have gone home to their families. The gnome and his partner have switched off their transistors and are smoking and talking to Joycie. The pinball machine has been dragged to a far corner to allow more room for four snooker players who keep saying 'fuck it' after every shot. They leave their cigarettes burning on the edge of the table, knowing the publican will never say a word. They are all in their late twenties and each one drinks more in one night than the gnome would in a week.

The cues shunt into the balls, which cannon across the table smacking each other with a noise like chipping porcelain. Alec watches their faces while they make their shots. One of them talks to the white ball as if it were his girlfriend. 'C'mon sweetheart, you can do it for Artie,' he says. Two more beers arrive.

'I don't think I enjoy my job anymore,' Alec says.

'I'm not surprised — happiest day of my life was leaving school, you couldn't drag me back.'

'Are you happy, Miles?'

'Are you kidding? Who wouldn't be? I've got it made; my own business, great bird. You'll be all right. Have a couple of sickies — go fishing or flying or something. Go away for a few days — always works for me. I've got to have a piss.'

Alec watches the snooker players. The one who talks to the

cue ball is winning. Alec can see why. It is because he wants to win more than the others. He watches everyone's shots and doesn't joke like the others. He is focused, Alec thinks, like a telescope on the moon. How could this game mean so much to him: coloured balls rolling around a table and falling into holes, more often by accident than anything else? The serious player will win, Alec thinks, he will become *the best* snooker player in the group and maybe that will be enough for him, maybe that will be enough. Miles returns and swivels on his stool.

'Somebody's thrown up in the loo,' he says to Joycie.

'Wonderful,' she says, closing her eyes.

'Do you love her, Miles?' Alec asks, focusing on his friend's eyes.

'Who, Joycie?' Miles laughs.

'Whoever made that disgusting mess in the toilet, would he kindly come and get this mop.' Joycie's voice carries through the pub. No one makes eye contact with her, like schoolchildren avoiding being singled out.

'Deirdre.'

'What's wrong with you, Alec, you really do need a holiday, mate. Although how a schoolie could need more holidays beats me.'

'I'll leave the mop over here,' Joycie says. 'And the naughty boy can come and get it.' A couple of snooker players laugh.

'Do you love Deirdre, Miles?'

'Give it a break, Alec, I don't know.'

'Are you going to get engaged?'

'I suppose so. What about you and Kate?'

'I don't love her, Miles.'

'Jesus Christ, have another drink.'

The snooker game behind them is over. The one who turned the white ball into his girlfriend has won. His face is relaxed and he moves slowly and appears to be noticing the other players for the first time since the game began. The others dip into their pockets and hand him some coins.

'I told Kate.'

'Oh shit, Alec. Jesus, I don't know, maybe you're having a breakdown or something, maybe you should see someone. I know you're in the business but they say doctors never know when they're sick.'

'And drunks never think they're drunk.'

'That's right.'

'Kate's mother came to see me afterwards. She said Kate was thinking about staying in Canberra after her course finished. I think she was relieved — Kate's mother, she was actually quite nice to me.'

'Well, it's her loss, mate.'

Alec looks along the bar and makes eye contact with the gnome. From this distance the gnome's eyes are the colour of his beer. Alec imagines what he may have been like as a child. He pictures a classroom. At the back sits the gnome with his one friend. He is not good at schoolwork, he is not popular, nor is he good-looking. He plays football but only fairly, and is, for much of his school life, invisible. He is not remembered by teachers or other students — there are no reunions he is called to, and he is seldom pointed out in the class photo. His name could be Barry or Ian and perhaps he let go of everything before he actually ever got a hold.

'I'm going, Miles.'

'Where?'

'To see a foreign lady.'

'I'll come.'

'No, on my own.'

'Can you drive?'

'Yes.'

'You sure?'

'Yes.'

'All right. Jesus, Deirdre'll drop dead to see me this bloody early.'

'I'm sorry, Miles.'

'It's okay.'

'I'll give you a call next week.'

'Okay, mate. Watch out for the foreign lady.'

'I'll see you later.'

'See you.'

'Bye.'

31

In the car, Alec knows he has drunk too much to go to Anik's directly, yet he knows that it is the alcohol that is producing his courage to go at all. He smiles at the idea of alcohol producing heroes — and then laughs out loud when he remembers a brand of beer actually called 'Courage'. More than likely, it peels back fear that protects as well as seals in, he muses: like orange peel. Imagine brave little oranges hanging naked from trees.

How drunk is he? What is he doing driving to Anik Pendraud's house — not Jack's, but Anik's? What in hell will he say when she opens the door? 'Hi, Anik, I was just driving by, half-tanked, and I thought I'd drop in and we could put old Erik Satie on and we could make love.' Wonderful. Should impress the hell out of her. She will say 'Come in,' of course, and she will say, 'Jacques,' how she says, Jacques, 'He is in bed.' But I haven't come to see Jacques, or Jack. I have come to see you.

Alec stops the car alongside a small park. He gets out jerkily and looks at the stars.

There is a small timber shelter with seats and a table for picnickers on the edge of the neatly trimmed grass. He slides along the bench seat, lights a cigarette and leans forward on the table.

'Got a spare one, mate?'

With a jerk, Alec drops his cigarette. The voice coming from the seat on the other side of the table takes shape. It is an old bum, who was lying prone on the bench seat. He appears less drunk than Alec as he sits upright. Alec gives him a cigarette and lights it.

'Thanks, mate, nice night for sutting.'

Alec picks up his cigarette and dusts it off.

'You bun drunkun?' the bum asks.

'Uh huh.'

'Haven't got a spare one on you, have you?'

'No, mate, sorry.'

'That's okay.'

'You New Zealander?'

'Yes, how'd you know?'

'Fush and chups — it's the "i" sound.'

'I've bun here twenty years, now.'

'I've never been to New Zealand.'

'Beautiful place. The South Island, I come from.'

'I've heard that.'

'I've got a place there, you know.'

'Good on you, mate.'

'No, really I have.'

'Why don't you go back?'

'Oh, well, ut's never that sumple, us ut?'

'I don't know.'

'I thunk about ut, though. Every day I thunk about ut. I thunk about ut more now than I dud when I was luving there.'

'Life's funny like that.'

'Ut us, usn't ut. You couldn't spare a few cugs for later, could you?'

'Have the packet, mate — it's Saturday, I always give 'em up on Saturday.'

'Thanks. Look, you haven't got a few bob to spare, have you?'

Alec pulls his wallet out of his back pocket and gives the old man a handful of notes. The man stuffs them quickly into his coat pocket and slides along the bench hurriedly. Unsteadily, he stands and begins to walk away.

'Thanks, mate,' he says.

'But I'm not adopting you,' Alec calls to him and laughs. The old man stops and turns his good ear towards Alec.

'What?'

'I said I'm not adopting you, okay?'

'Go to buggery — you go to buggery,' he sings out as he hurries out of Alec's range.

'Get stuffed, yourself,' Alec mumbles to himself. He wonders whether giving him money is a favour to the bum or himself. Alec laughs about the old man still holding up pride like his trousers with the frayed string around the waist.

Alec lights another cigarette. And Jack, what is it I can do for you, Jack? I'm supposed to know, I'm supposed to help. But I don't know, Jack, and I don't help, and I was the best in the class.

Dark eyes, deep heart.

'Anik.'

'Alec.'

'I was passing by and I thought I'd drop in.'

'Come in.'

'I was with my friend Miles Fenton . . .'

'Would you like a drink?'

'Ah, no thanks.'

'Jacques, he is in bed.'

'I haven't come to see Jacques or Jack. I have come to see you.'

Anik's body feels exactly as Alec knew it would — hardly touched by the sun, soft, with poor muscle tone. From the corner of the room Satie plays impressionist notes. Anik folds around his body with her legs and arms. He rises and falls with the music, moving into her, watching her face.

'I love you,' he says.

The night is still and clear. The park is empty but fringed by the yellowish window lights of red brick homes on all sides. Houses full of people and food smells and music and toilet cleansers and secret dreams and hopeless hopes: naked oranges in the night.

32

New Guinea 1968

Suli has called me a sorceress again, and he does not speak softly, he shouts at me. His anger turns his face away from me and sharpens his body against me. I have learnt the purpose of anger from watching the children play: it is fashioned like the head of the stone axe, to wedge between the wants of another and those of oneself. I choose not to be separated from what I want by Suli's anger. He has screamed in my face and thrown a stone at me. He has refused to sit near me in the schoolhouse and still I persist. I will watch his man-coming ceremony, even though it is forbidden. I tell him that I will hide amongst the kunai and it will never be known that the eyes of a meri have been with them.

'I will never tell you where it is,' he shouts at me. For a long time, I do not answer, as I run to keep up with his angry legs along the track.

'You are sanguma,' he calls back to me, and spits at my feet.

'And you are a deceiver.'

He stops in front of me and turns.

'What do you say?' He stands ready to hit me.

'The mission says that a Christian must not take his man-coming,' I tell him. Suli's eyes widen and then narrow like a hungry bird. We both stand staring as if we had not ever properly looked on each other. 'How can you walk two paths?' I ask.

'I do not walk them at the same time, meri.'

'Then I will ask at the mission about those who wish to become ministers and the . . .'

'No!'

'Then I will watch your coming.'

'You are longlong, you are mad . . . they would kill you.'

'I would not be seen in the kunai — I know where it is done — by the river, in the wetlands.'

'You are sanguma, you should not know this.' Suli sits down on the track with his fists tight. 'Why do you want to know such things?'

Within myself, I try to answer Suli's question, but I do not know why.

I wait quietly for Suli to tell me when he and the other two boys will come from the men's haus and go to the secret site at the river. He tells me of the day, and of the sound of the mystical forest bird that he and the other boys will wait for, and there is nothing more that he knows.

'If they find you — you cannot say that I told you.'

'They will not find me,' I say.

33

Australia 1964

Jack slips quietly through the back door of the house and into the kitchen. David Johnston had arranged to meet him at the park to try Jack's football, but David never showed up. Jack waited an hour and then went to the Johnstons' house. Mrs. Johnston said that David had gone off with two other boys from school on their bikes.

Jack finds an apple on top of the refrigerator and uses the long carving knife to begin peeling it. He cuts his thumb slightly as the cumbersome blade slides off the apple skin. He puts his thumb in his mouth, drops the apple onto the floor and grinds his heel up and down and round and round into it, mashing it into the quarry tiles of the floor.

His body is sticking with sweat from running as fast as he could back from David Johnston's house. He tries to understand why David didn't wait for him. It is puzzling, like the cut on his thumb. He places the knife edge on his thumb and presses, watching the flesh go white along the point of contact. He imagines sliding the knife along as it presses into his skin, and the blade slicing down to the white bone and the thumb splitting into two halves.

From the front door, he hears voices. One of them sounds like his father. He begins to walk to the door to see and then decides to stop.

'Is Jack home?' It is his father.

'No, he has gone to play with his friend,' his mother answers.

'Good. I have Damian with me, can we come in?'

'Yes, of course.'

'Anik, this is Damian Hall; alas, he does not speak French.'

Jack hears them sitting in the lounge chairs. Some of the words are difficult for him to hear and he strains towards the door. His father sounds to be sitting opposite his mother and alongside his friend.

'I wanted the two of you to meet,' Jack's father says. 'I talk about you so often to Damian that he must wonder whether you are real or a figment of my imagination.'

Jack opens the door a fraction. He sees the back of his father's head above the lounge, and his mother sitting opposite.

'I have been worried, Anik, about Jack. Since he saw us, he has been different.'

'What do you mean — saw us?'

'He didn't tell you?' There is a silence.

In the kitchen, Jack opens the broom cupboard, climbs in and shuts the door. He holds his fists against his ears. The knife handle presses against the right side of his face. The voices from the lounge room can still be heard.

'Jack saw us together, Damian and I.'

Damian is embarrassed and speaks to Anik as he stares at the floor.

'He didn't say a thing. He just stood in the doorway, staring and staring — I can still see his eyes.' Damian frowns at the floor.

'What did he do?' Anik's voice sounds steady in the room.

'Nothing, he just turned around and left.'

'When did this happen?'

'About two months ago.'

'And you tell me only now?'

'I'm sorry, Anik, I thought Jack would have said something.'

'What did he see, Jean? Were you . . . ?'

'With Damian, yes.'

'He saw you both?'

'Yes.'

'Did you speak to him?'

'No, I couldn't. He left so quickly.'

'Later, you could have spoken to him later.'

Jean looks away from Anik's eyes. Damian does not move. Anik is angry. 'What do you want to do about it?' she asks.

'I want to talk to him.'

'And tell him what?'

'I want to explain as best I can.'

In the cupboard, Jack has uncovered his ears; he cannot stop himself from listening through the louvred slats of the broom cupboard doors.

'I am going back to Paris with Damian, Anik.'

Damian cuts in gently, 'We both think it's the best solution.'

'It is not good, how things are,' says Jack's father.

'And what will you tell Jacques?'

'I will tell him as much of the truth as I can.'

'He still believes we will come together again.' Anik's voice is strained.

'Yes, I know.'

'We must tell him together. There is a friend of Jacques from his school, a counsellor, I will speak with him.'

'Is he having problems at school?'

'Yes.'

'I didn't know.'

'There is much you do not know about him.' There is a metallic edge to her voice.

'Damian,' Jean asks quietly. 'Could you go to the kitchen, it is in there, and make some coffee, please? I will speak with Anik for a little while.'

'The coffee and cups are in the cupboard above the sink,' Anik says politely.

Anik watches Damian move across the room. He is obviously grateful to escape further embarrassment. Anik is surprised at how young he is. It must have taken quite a lot of courage to come here, she thinks. Jean is telling her about his plans, and how Jacques will be able to visit him, and herself as well, of course. Anik remembers Jean before they were married: tall and thin and confident. She met him at university, through a mutual friend who described him as gentle and sensitive. In the beginning, she pursued him with subtlety, and then they were together almost every possible moment, discussing plans, describing their love, touching each other. There was seldom a need for sex — they talked and walked and dreamed of how they would reform a stupid world. They smoked and drank together and laughed and argued about Fedor Mikhailovich Dostoevsky, and Balzac and Flaubert, as if they understood them. And if they were apart they were unhappy. Their friends said that they looked good together. And they laughed and raged and felt sure the world would bend under the weight of all the things they had learned. Anik became pregnant and Jean wanted her to have an abortion but she refused, left university and the baby was stillborn. Jean left university and married her, and for a while they were happy. Flouting the rules; living in rich poverty; working at meaningless jobs; meeting the real world. But over the years, the talk dried up, the ideas were reshaped, and a 'knowing' filled the departed space of innocence. Jacques was born. Friends changed, and plans faded. And the love? Neither of them noticed: the lake in the desert — was it ever really there?

Jean told her of his lover, and they cried together and came to Australia to begin again. For a moment, like the first splash of paint on a new canvas, there were possibilities and new plans; and then Damian. And it was over.

Damian steps into the kitchen. Jack watches him through the louvres. He is short and thin and he is the man Jack remembers seeing in bed with his father. From the lounge, Jack thinks he can hear his mother walking across the room as his father speaks softly, in low tones. He watches Damian find coffee and the cups and fill the kettle and plug it in. Systematically, Damian pulls open drawers and eventually locates the one with the teaspoons. He leans with his back against the sink. Jack looks at his face. He feels a tightness in the skin across his cheekbones. There is a roaring in his ears, like being dumped in the surf; in his mouth, a taste of salt. The muscles in his legs and arms feel loaded, coiled. Sweat runs down his thumping chest from the dark heat of the cupboard.

Damian notices the crushed apple on the floor near the refrigerator and bends down to inspect it. He looks at the bowl of fruit on top and frowns. He looks around the room and heads for the broom cupboard.

Inside, Jack curls up tight. Damian's face comes close to Jack's through the slats of the door. He pulls it open and Jack, in one movement, springs upwards from his crouching position and watches the knife in his hand extend like a Nazi salute and enter Damian's throat through his Adam's apple, the point coming out the other side of his neck. Jack's thumb and finger touch Damian's flesh and he lets go the handle as if it were hot. He is sprayed across the eyes with blood. Damian does not make a sound, his eyes are startled and his hands fly up and clutch at the knife. His fingers shake in disbelief at what they feel. He sees Jack's face, terrified. There are bubbles of blood popping with air from his neck.

For some seconds they stare at each other, as if waiting for this blur of impossibility to pass. Damian tries to stand up, but flops to one side. He watches his blood pumping across the floor and running in rivulets along the cement joints in the tiles. There is no energy left for him to do anything but watch the flood.

Jack jumps over Damian's chest and runs to the kitchen door. His father and mother are speaking French. His mother sees him and leaps to her feet.

34

New Guinea 1968

Amongst the long kunai at the edge of the wetlands, I lie and wait. I have walked to the river at night so that I will not be seen. Water has squeezed from the ground where my body touches, and the coldness of the early morning seeps through to my bones. Many times I think I hear the men and Suli coming, but it is a bird or a frog. The mist has moved up the mountain and here the air is still and clear. I begin to wonder why it is that I came, and then I see them along the river bank — a line of middle men. They move softly through the bush, one behind the other.

I look at the crushed grass that marks my own path to where I lie. Most of it stands tall again and would not point to me. I see Suli, as the men form a circle near the river and sit. My mouth is dry and my belly twists inside.

I would go now, if I could move without being seen. I see the men in slices, through the grass. They sit and smoke and some of their words come to me. My father would be angry with me for what I do.

I see the heads of all those by the river turn as one towards a call from the bush. It is the mystical forest bird. The circle of men stand up and cease their talking. The sound is beautiful to hear and floats across the tips of the grass through the damp air of the morning. It is the sound that no meri can hear — but I hear it, and I am a meri. The music of the bird comes closer from the forest and I am between it and the men on the river bank.

At the edge of the trees, before the kunai begins, it stops moving. I want to look but I am afraid to lift my head. The bird is on a pathway to the river clearing and it will pass close by me. Between the notes, I hear the grass bend under the feet of the bird. I stop my breath and shrink into the mud. The music carries a sadness which speaks for the beauty of the valley. I see the legs of the bird pass by me. My trapped breath hurts my chest. The legs are not those of a bird. I want to scream out. My body is stone-like. They are the legs of a middle man of the line. To his mouth he holds tiny bamboo rods, bound together with vine in the shape of a flute. It is this that makes the bird noise. With his eyes on the circle of men by the river, he does not see me as he passes.

The group at the river make welcoming shouts and leap into the air, encircling the flute player. They dance and chant to the music as they point at and tease Suli and the other two boys. I feel the confusion that must be with Suli as he learns the truth of the mystical bird, who flew so high in our thoughts. I watch the boys touch the flutes and each, in turn, attempts to blow music from them while the men laugh.

I am angry that this truth has been kept from me for so long but I am repaid by the knowing, as if I had stolen something from all of them.

The boys cannot play the flutes and are told that when they are men they will be taught the secret. To hear their words clearly, I crawl closer to the river. I watch the tops of the kunai as I pass so that the movement is no more than the push of the wind.

From the bush I hear drums that move closer to the men at the river. I see three men covered in white clay who step into the clearing. On their belts they have tied small bundles of sharp-edged tiwi grass. They stop, each one in front of a boy. The other men move to form a circle and sit like a pig fence around the boys. The white clay men throw down their drums and take up a bundle of tied grass. One of them shouts at the river. His words cause the boys to shiver.

'You have eaten poison. Poison mun-blood!'

The boys look at each other and I can see that they do not understand. The clay man continues.

'That swam like a snake in the belly of your mother!'

The boys move closer together.

'Before you are born — you are poisoned,' the clay man shouts. 'And you must be cleansed.'

Suli seems to stare at the place where I lie, as if he knows I am here. I see fear in his eyes. The three clay men hold the bundles of grass out in front of them and the shouting one dances around the boys, stops and then stabs the knife-edged bundle hard into his own nose. He works the green blades in and out of his nostrils, and the blood comes, gushing down over his lips and chin and down his chest. Suli's eyes are wide with fright. He looks at the circle of men and back at the bleeding clay man who points a fresh bundle of grass blades at him. The blood has mixed with the white on the chest of the clay man. Suli cannot reach for the grass, he is tight with fear. Two men from the circle stand quickly and move towards him. He is pushed to the ground and his arms are held back. The clay man tears off Suli's belt and tanket leaves. He is naked on the ground as the grass thrusts into the soft flesh inside his nose. He screams before the blood rushes out and covers his teeth. In time he stops struggling but the men holding him have not let his arms go. The clay man has not finished, he points to Suli's penis and holds it between his thumb and finger. I hear the clay man's talk. He says that Suli's penis will not grow and his seed will not come unless a tissue in his body is broken. From his belt the clay man pulls a bent piece of cane and waves it across Suli's face. Suli is like a pig before the sing-sing, and I wish that I had not come. I think that I should not see these things, that perhaps I will become sick. Perhaps I am longlong as Suli says, or worse, that I am sanguma. And yet, I watch, there is something to be known here, which comes closer, like the sun before it is seen in the morning.

The clay man swoops on Suli with his cane hook and pushes it down his throat. Suli's eyes go large as he chokes. The clay man works the cane up and down. I can see where it pushes the skin on Suli's neck outwards as it searches to break the tissue which blocks his growth.

With great strength, Suli breaks from the men holding his arms, the top of his body leaps upwards and from his throat spurts a foul stream of half-eaten taro and blood. I look for pieces of the tissue, as Suli writhes back and forth. I see none.

The sun is about to appear over the edge of the valley.

Suli stops jerking and spilling his stomach onto the ground. There is no tissue. The sun fires its first arrows. There is no tissue on the ground and the clay man has stopped, satisfied. He is chanting a strange song about an ancient enemy.

The sun will soon be seen. There is no tissue.

I listen to the words of the song that tell the boys they must be clean for one year, that they must not take food from the hands of a meri, nor can they eat lizards, snakes or frogs. Each morning of the moon change, before the sun, they must bleed their noses and wash in the cold river water and they must not go up a meri or touch her body.

Like the sun lifting the night the knowledge comes to me: the men who hide themselves from meris, who count their pigs and fight for land, who buy wives to plant their gardens and grow their picaninis; these men hide by the river and tear their bodies to bleed like meris. They are men by becoming meris. I have the power of knowing.

The song changes to a higher, more urgent note. The other men stop singing, and only one clay man continues. Not one man or boy moves by the river. The song sits in the air and tells how our line, the people of Tabunak, must eat the body of another; a strong man, a master spirit, whose strength will pass to us from the marrow in his bones: who eats another, becomes both men. The clay man's voice skims across the water and through the grass and disappears high up into the valley.

'He comes,' the clay man sings. 'One who brings the future — and he will bring strength back to our line.'

The singing stops. There is no movement. I do not understand who it is the clay man says that we must eat.

From the circle, I see a middle man stand and point towards me. I stop my breath with fear. I see that I have risen higher in the grass than I should have. I sink to the ground, but it is too late. Two of the men are running towards me.

35

Australia 1964

Alec is surprised at how calm he remains while listening to Anik on the telephone. It is as if the information on Jack, like a sick patient, is ushered into an insulated waiting room. Jack has been placed in a children's centre operated by the Department of Child Welfare. Alec knows it as Jindawarra House. He knows the superintendent.

Anik's voice on the phone is thin and desperate. She has been given limited access to Jack for 48 hours. Alec listens. He isn't quite sure what he is feeling; a need to help Jack — a flush of energy channelled into thought.

'I know the superintendent there,' he says. 'I may be able to see Jack.'

'Could you, Alec, please?' Anik's voice rises. 'I don't want him to be afraid and alone, I feel . . . I am afraid for Jacques.'

36

'What happened, Jack?'

'I don't know, Alec, can I go home?'

'No, you'll have to stay here for a while — I don't know for how long. Your mother's coming to see you at four o'clock tomorrow.'

Jack's eyes begin to fill.

'Is he? . . . did he . . . ?'

'Yes, he's dead.'

'They wouldn't tell me.'

Jack takes a slow, deep breath; his chest and upper body are shaking. In the corridor outside, footsteps clack along the polished vinyl floor. There is a large clock on the wall of the room which is an imitation of an old railway clock with Roman numerals; its ticking expands to fill the room.

'Did you mean to do it, Jack?'

'I don't know, I just . . . when he opened the door, I just jumped out and there he was . . . and the knife . . . was . . . was . . . sticking out of his neck. What will they do to me, Alec?'

'I'm not sure, they'll probably keep you here for a few days and some people will come and talk to you.'

'Will they give me the cane?'

'No.'

'David wasn't home.'

'What do you mean, Jack?'

'We were supposed to have some kicks with my footie.'

'David Johnston?'

'He said he'd meet me, but he didn't come.'

'This is before . . .?'

'He probably forgot.'

'Probably.'

'He's always forgetting.'

Outside, the night is moonless; there is a Liquidambar tree close enough to the window for the electric light to show some of its jagged leaves. The clock ticks into the neatness of the room and Alec feels that both he and Jack upset the balance somehow; that a room such as this should belong to a Jesuit priest or a nursing sister or someone as contained as itself.

'Are you hungry?'

'No, they gave me a pie and chips. Can you stay here with me?'

'No, they won't allow that.'

'I don't like it here.'

'Me neither.' Jack smiles.

'Have they got a playground?' Jack asks.

'Yes, a good one, with a tennis court and a pool.'

'What will they do with me, Alec?'

'Break your legs off and beat your head in with the stumps.' Jack tries to smile. Alec cannot stop himself, knowing clearly what he is about to do. 'Maybe what happened, Jack,' he says, 'was that he tripped, in the kitchen, I mean, and he fell on the knife . . . maybe you thought he was breaking into the house . . . maybe that's what happened, Jack — you thought he was a robber, or something, and you held the knife at him and he tripped and fell forward onto it.'

Alec is conscious of the sliding peephole cut into the door. Someone in the corridor would check the room regularly, every fifteen minutes. A sliding sound and an eye — Jack had already become accustomed to it.

'Let's get you into bed, eh?'

Jack has his school case with clothes and pyjamas.

'Would you like me to get you a pad and a pen? A writer can't be left too long without his equipment.' And Alec sits on the bed as Jack lies there.

Alec feels his uselessness again; could anyone ever help anyone else? Did we all just bump around each other like coloured balls on green felt — rolling and smacking into each other and sending each other in different directions? Rolling and smacking, rolling and smacking.

'I'll stay until you go to sleep, Jack.'

37

Alec notices that Anik has drunk too much again, her face is withdrawn. He tells her that Jack is all right and that he will probably be released in a few days. She looks towards the kitchen door where she first saw Jack covered in blood. She asks Alec what will happen. He tells her that a psychiatrist will make out a report and the case will go to court and a decision will be made about what to do with Jack.

Anik sits and talks while Alec paces around the room.

'Did he mean to do it?' Anik asks as if Alec is not really present.

'I don't know.'

'He has always been . . . different . . . so different. I have tried many things with him . . . and with Jean . . . sometimes I would wish that I had not had him. He has taken so many years . . . and now he is not here, I want him back. I am like the dog who never accepts the limits of his chain.'

Anik curls forward, wrapping her arms around her legs. Alec, staring at the curving expanse of her back, steps behind the chair and begins to massage the rigid muscles in her neck and shoulders.

'Do you understand why this has happened?' Anik leans her head back to face Alec, and spills her drink. 'You do, don't you? But you have failed to save us . . . Jacques and I are like the stupid dog who runs and chokes, runs and chokes.'

38

Jack's head is barely visible between Anik and Jean at the front door of the courtroom. There is no natural light entering the room. The magistrate's raised bench of polished veneer dominates the room and forces those in the front to tilt their heads back. It is a hearing closed to the public, but Alec approaches the attendant carrying a briefcase and an armful of papers in a brown manila folder. He glances impatiently at his watch and intimidates the attendant who holds the door open for him. Alec sits at the rear of the courtroom noticing the stale air of the room as he slides along the vinyl seat.

At the front, the magistrate is speaking with the Pendrauds' legal representative in a low voice — as if the Pendrauds are present only as cardboard cutouts. Officers from the Department of Child Welfare and Health Department sit patiently across the aisle from Anik. Near the magistrate, and in front of two slumped Australian flags that have never flown, sits a court reporter huddled over his pad. It is the third and final court appearance for Jack. Alec has not been permitted to visit him since the first night, when a special report was filed regarding Alec's conversation with Jack.

The magistrate calls the Child Welfare Officer and psychiatrist to his bench and continues speaking in a whispering voice. Alec stares at the back of Anik's head, willing her to turn around and smile at him — to see her face. His stomach is empty and makes loud noises of complaint. The talk at the front finishes and the group return to their seats. The magistrate begins speaking to the Pendraud family.

'Mr. and Mrs. Pendraud, and Jack, previously the court has established and recorded a verdict of death by manslaughter in the circumstances of Mr. Damian Hall, and this hearing has determined that some responsibility exists for Jack Pendraud, who is eleven and not liable under law. The degree of culpability has not been determined satisfactorily. From discussions with relevant child specialists from the various Government departments, it appears that some element of emotional disorder exists for Jack. The basis for this disorder is believed to stem from conflict surrounding the separated living arrangements of you, his parents, Mr. and Mrs. Pendraud. It is not a pleasant duty of this court to direct custody of such a young child to the care of the state; however, it is in the court's power, and indeed its responsibility, to ensure that the best interests of both the public and the child are protected. During discussions with you, Mr. and Mrs. Pendraud, expressions of your desire to reunite the family have been taken into account. A broken home is seen as far from the ideal setting to raise this boy and it is therefore ordered by this court that custody of Jack Pendraud shall rest with the state while the parents, Jean and Anik Pendraud, are living apart or are deemed to be separated. However, custody of Jack will be reassigned to you, and will remain with you, Mr. and Mrs. Pendraud, provided there is an undertaking on your part that you will resume living together as a family unit. The court acknowledges the family's intention of returning to France, and passport applications will not be opposed.'

Anik turns around and sees Alec at the back of the room.

39

Alec is surprised to hear Jack's voice on the telephone.

'Does your mother know you are calling, Jack?'

'No, she's having a bath.'

'How are you going?'

'All right.'

'How is she?'

'Okay.'

'That's good.'

'Dad's going to live with us now — but we're going back to France.'

'Are you?'

'I don't want to go, and I can't speak hardly any French.'

'You'll probably learn it very quickly.'

'You could come with us, Alec.'

'To France?'

'You wouldn't have to get a job — my grandfather has got plenty of money.'

'I can't speak any French at all.'

'You can learn, too.'

'Thanks, Jack.'

'I want you to come, Alec.'

'I know that, Jack — maybe I'll come and visit.'

'Would you?'

'Yes.'

'Promise?'

40

'Alec?'

'Yes.'

'I saw you at the back of the courtroom.'

'I told the attendant I was with the Child Welfare Department.'

'That was clever.'

'How's Jack?'

'He's very quiet.'

'What will you do now?'

'Jean is here, he is talking about returning to France.'

'Jack told me.'

'I should have realised . . .'

'While you were having a bath, yesterday.'

'He wants you to come with us.'

'I can't speak French.'

'Jacques says you could learn.'

Alec can hear his breath increasing its strength. The hand holding the receiver is wet with sweat.

'You could stay,' he says.

'Yes, with great difficulty for Jacques.'

Outside, Alec becomes aware of the street traffic noise that he realises must have always been there.

'How are you feeling?' he asks.

'I am quite calm, really — I have not been drinking.'

'Do you want to go back to France?'

'No.'

'But you are going?'

'Jacques couldn't go back to his school — we would have to move anyway, and there would need to be new work — new jobs, for Jean and myself.'

'I'll miss you.'

'And I will . . . we will miss you.'

'I still have your books.'

'I would like you to keep them . . . Alec?'

'Yes?'

'I have appreciated what you have done for us.'

So softly, that Alec isn't certain it is said at all: 'I love you.'

'I can't see you again, Alec,' she says.

41

New Guinea 1968

I am slow to rise to my feet. The swamp water has spread through my bones and my legs do not bend easily. The two men by the river stop running when they see me stand. They are shocked and cry out to the others in confusion. All of the heads at the river turn towards me. As I turn to run, I see Suli's face like a falling leaf, coloured with blood and vomit. Behind me there is a roar of the men who come after me.

I run, splashing through pools of floating weed and swamp flowers. I hear the feet of the men splashing and pounding behind me. My legs have filled too much with the cold, and the pain tells me to stop as I run. I head towards the safety of the forest, where I can hide amongst the trees and bushes, and climb away up the side of the mountain. The sounds behind me are closer. I am like the muruk in front of its killers, whose legs and wings beat through the air to keep ahead, to delay. I have listened to the last cry of the muruk; a call to its mate.

I would pull the forest to me. I would give back the knowledge I have gained for the safety of the bush. I want my father. I hear my voice crying out his name. The call runs ahead of me, skimming the water and reaching into the edge of trees. I am afraid to die.

I know that many of the men behind me carry axes in their belts. I can hear their hunters' breath as they come closer. Like the muruk, I cannot outrun them. My knowledge will not help me here. I stop running and turn to face them.

The fastest runners reach me first. They stop as I look at them and they turn their heads back to the others. I thrust my hands under the laplap between my legs, as the middle men push past the young men closest to me.

'I am in blood!' I shout.

Several of the closest men step backwards.

'Do not believe her — she is lying.' It is Kaio who speaks. A middle man takes an axe from his belt. Under my laplap, I hook the nail of my thumb under the nail of a finger. I lift the nail in a quick flicking movement, and feel it tear away the skin. The pain makes me want to cry out but I do not open my mouth as the damp spreads along my finger and drips down my hand and into the laplap. I am surprised how much there is. I dip my fingers into its warmth and pull out my hand for the men to see.

There is a gasp of fear from those that can see.

'She is sanguma,' one of them says.

'Cut her,' says another.

'No, you will be followed by her masalai.'

'A burial hole, then, let the ground kill her.'

Those closest to me step aside to allow the clay man through. He moves towards me, and I see that it is Wahgi.

'She is longlong since the dying of her father and mother,' he says as he looks at me. I feel that he can see the torn fingernail.

'She will tell what she has seen,' Kaio shouts out from the back of the group.

'And who will believe the words of a longlong meri, who goes to the mission school like a boy and lives by herself?' Wahgi looks at the faces of the others as he speaks. No talk comes from the other men.

'Why do you hide in the kunai?' Wahgi asks me.

My head beats inside as I hear Wahgi's words. I see Suli, rigid with terror at one side of the group. I roll my eyes back into my head and begin to shake the fingers with the blood. Small drops spray about me. The front men leap backwards, cursing and yelping. I spit at them and fall to the ground.

'She is sanguma,' a voice shouts.

'She is longlong,' the Tul-Tul calls.

Wahgi lifts me to my feet by my hair. He turns to the others.

'If she tells what she has seen and heard, then she is truly sanguma, and I will be the one to fill her mouth with earth.' Wahgi looks at each man's face in turn and they look away. He lets go my hair.

'Go!' he tells me. 'And speak to no one of what you have seen — or the hand of the masalai will choke the life from you in the night.'

And my feet are running, stamping into the soft soil across the ground and into the forest, and I have taken the knowledge with me; into the heart of the valley.

42

Australia 1964

Miles is quieter than usual, subdued by the airport's size and authority. He looks at Alec and wonders how he can remain so calm, outwardly at least.

'I suppose flying doesn't bother you?'

'No, not much.'

'What time do you get to Moresby?'

'About seven in the morning.'

'Be hot as hell.'

'Probably.'

'Maybe I'll come up and visit you after a while.'

'I'd like that, Miles.'

'Probably have to bring old Deirdre along now that we're practically shackled. She wanted to come here tonight, but I put my foot down.'

'The one with the shackles?'

'Ha ha.'

Seats around the terminal are beginning to fill with groups of travellers whose excited bubbles of talk float up towards the exposed steel trusses of the roof. Overhead there is a call for passengers for a flight to London. Alec and Miles both look towards the speakers.

'We had some good times, didn't we, Alec?'

'We did, Miles.'

'Remember Joycie?'

'Who could forget Joycie.'

'With the big . . . ears.' Miles laughs and shakes his head. 'Remember that fight we almost got into with that big Latvian bloke . . . ?'

'With the white beard?'

'Who would have thought anyone that old could be so strong . . .'

'And fast . . .'

'And vicious.' Miles and Alec laugh. 'I think I'll keep our Thursday nights going — I'll drink your share as well . . .'

Alec notices that Miles only looks at Alec's face when he is laughing. He thinks that there should be something to say; something significant that will make importance out of Miles's and Alec's hours together — like the framing of a painting. But the words do not come. And the picture remains unsigned — a throwaway print. Miles stands a little way from Alec, rocking backwards and forwards on the balls of his feet. And no words come.

'I think you'll make a good patrol officer.'

'Thanks, Miles.'

'Lying under a coconut tree . . .'

'No coconut trees in the Highlands.'

'Is that where you're going? Christ, they still run around naked up there — I saw it on a film on the ABC, what do you want to go there for?'

'It's where they posted me.'

'Oh, well, it's probably not as bad as the film made out.'

And there is quiet between them which makes Miles pull at his neck and look around and shift his weight from one leg to the other.

'I don't think there's much point in me staying to the bitter end, eh?'

'No, they'll call me up, soon.'

'Yes, well, I suppose this is it, mate. Best of luck.' Miles shakes Alec's hand.

'You too, Miles — I hope it all works out for you.'

'It will, mate, Deirdre'll insist on it.' Miles laughs. 'Look after yourself up there — and don't think I'm going to call you "Masta" when you come back.'

'I'll see you, Miles.'

'Yeh, I'll be off. See you, Alec.'

'Goodbye, Miles.'

Alec watches Miles stride across the terminal, one hand in his pocket. He stops at the automatic doors, turns, waves, salutes, and is gone.

Alec's flight to Port Moresby is called through the loudspeakers. He picks up his overnight bag and walks towards the Customs entrance. And there is Kate between him and the doors. He stops, puts down his bag and embraces her. Kate is close to tears. Alec begins to make a joke about Humphrey Bogart and Ingrid Bergman, but stops himself. There is nothing left for them to say, the words between them long exhausted.

There are others around them, holding onto each other, attempting to deny an ending like the edge of a mountain in darkness.

Alec squeezes Kate's hand, gives her a wink, and disappears through the doors.

Walk away from the wall and
say to yourself: now I see
the maze that confused me
when I stood so close.
Take comfort in its endless,
shrinking safety.
And in each step see less of
each stone, feel none of the
sun's heat captured in the
clay, and never again touch
the names carved into the
bricks by those who stood with
you in confusion, so close.

PART II

1

New Guinea April 3rd 1968

Under streak-lines of rain, the swamp appears joined to the clouds. Alec feels the metal tricounis of his boots dig into the bark of the logs floating on the surface. From Iumbis to Karakar, during the wet season it is always the same. Although the flat land is a welcome change from climbing rainforest mountains and the inevitable toe-gripping, mud-sliding crawl down the slopes where rushing water and black feet have exposed giant, twisted roots of trees and treacherous loose rock.

Water seeps and leaks through the thick woollen socks and sucks at the flesh of his instep at each stride. Even the old felt army hat is soaked through. The carriers of the patrol boxes are quiet — they have not sung together all day. Four of them have pretended to be sick, and have gone back to their houses. This has never happened to Alec before. There is always great pride at each village line to welcome the Government, in the form of the kiap. Only when Alec had threaded a bush pole through the handles of the boxes and lifted it to his shoulder did the embarrassed onlookers laughingly replace the four missing carriers, and take the weight from him.

Alec knows why they are not pleased. It is not the census, a time of family pride, to parade the new babies — to bury the dead in the kiap's books. He has happily counted their lives throughout the valley each year since arriving. The 'senus', they called it, as they wondered why the kiap would want to capture their names and days of births in giant books. So many of the Europeans' actions were a mystery to them in the beginning, but later there was always a purpose.

Alec's other purpose on this patrol is to tell them of pyrethrum, the tiny, daisy-like flower which can be turned by factories into a poison for insects. The flower can thrive amongst their sweet potato gardens at this high altitude. A flower which could be grown, picked and taken to the patrol post station — for cash. Round, silver money to be traded at mission stores for steel axes and cigarettes, for corned beef and tins of Fanta, and flat-bladed machetes.

To collect the pyrethrum flowers, there would need to be roads and bridges cut into the valley for trucks. And with the trucks will come many of the good things that the whites have made and worked for themselves. Alec knows that the old men and many of the middle men can see how such roads carved into the heart of the valley will bleed its strength and leave them powerless to new and relentless enemies. Alec knows it is the wealthy who have most to lose, and when he speaks to a line at each census gathering ground, he works hard to explain what will come, and how it is inevitable.

At Tabunak, the next census ground, it would be even more difficult. A strong old man, Parap, must be taken back to the patrol post station to face the district court for killing his wife. Her body had been carried to the station with the axe still embedded in her spine. Parap found her with another man and had to kill her, or lose face. Parap would present himself at the census, Alec knew, and he would go with him readily enough, back to the patrol post — and it would be just one more instance of the increasing power of the Government over the big men of the valley.

On the high ground at Karakar, Alec slips his hand inside his shorts, searching carefully for leeches. He has never found one at this altitude, the temperature too cold, but the horror stories still lurk from training at Moresby of the cadet patrol officer who had the leech inside his penis.

The carriers sit and smoke. Some of the younger men, arms around each other's shoulders, laugh and joke. Tarus, Alec's interpreter, approaches and squats down near Alec.

'Masta, there is talk coming up from the valley, from Tabunak — they say that they do not want the white flower in their gardens.'

'Then we shall have to convince them.'

'And Parap, the one who has cut his meri, has begun to buy a new bride.'

'What does that mean, Tarus?'

'He does not expect that he will come with us to the station.'

'We might have to convince him as well.'

'Masta, could we go around Tabunak?'

Alec watches Edith, the district nurse, catch up. Across the swamp, she has been carried on a canvas bed sleeve. As they set her down, she smiles at the carriers.

'God, I think I feel seasick. How much further to Tabunak?'

'Four or five hours.'

2

The kiap sits at his table which has legs that cross over and fold out underneath. I remember him from before, when I stood with my father and mother and I heard him call my name. I did not know then how he could know my name but now I can write it myself and I can read the label on his book — 'Tabunak'. I have practised some English words to say to him when my family name is called.

Behind the kiap's rest haus I can see the little doctor putting medicine in the arms of the babies through little holes she makes, and they cry out and twist in their mothers' arms. The kiap says this can stop the coughing death. Some meris will not bring their picaninis, even though the kiap's word has been sent out.

I listen to the voice of the kiap as the whole line sits in the sun on the ground sing-sing. He smiles at each family as he calls them to his table. The little children hide behind their mothers' legs and the men stand proudly in front. The kiap cannot speak our language and needs his man, a tanim-tok, to change the words for his ears. When the names of the whole line have been called and the census books are full with new babies and free of the dead, he will lock them in his iron box and sit in his rest haus. He will smoke, and talk with the old men and the middle men, and listen to the courts — the fights for land and pigs — and he will judge who is right.

I hear my father's name from the mouth of the kiap, and my courage to speak to him flies out of my heart like a hunted forest pigeon. I stand and walk to the table. The kiap calls the name of my father and my mother and I say nothing. I stand in front of him. The talking noise of the whole line has gone quiet as the kiap looks at me. In their silence I feel the line's disapproval like heat before the storm rains. I am shamed in front of the line — there is no one to stand up with me and I have no words, only long tears that run inside my nose and over my lips and down my breasts and stomach. Tears that would fall into and fill the kiap's book.

Tears, my father said, are like the smoke from boiling water: the dreams of pain, escaping.

3

Alec looks out of the rest house doorway into the night. He rubs at the smoke in his eyes, knowing that the whites will be red and the red will be sore tomorrow. He wonders why they have never understood about chimneys. The tanim-tok has told him that they harden shields and arrow points by leaving them tied to the ceiling above the cooking fire to smoke-blacken. He thinks about his eyes going hard — like cartilage or gristle — and turning black. He turns from the doorway.

Edith is stretched across her bed sleeve, exhausted. Her first long patrol. Alec looks at her sprawled on the canvas. He will massage her neck and shoulders tonight. It is something they do for each other most nights of the patrol; the smoothing of muscles that clot together during the day, like strung beads.

They speak of their day: his census, the court cases, her vaccinations. She flares and rages about the women who will not bring their babies to the little doctor's pricking. He listens patiently, imagining her neck muscles twisting. He turns the sweet potatoes at the edge of the fire.

'Two thirds of them will die, you know, Alec — the babies, I mean,' she says.

'Little fingers.'

'What?' She turns her head to face him.

'The mothers,' he says, holding up his little finger, 'cut off one joint when their baby dies.'

'Jesus Christ,' she shakes her head: tension down the spine, flesh stretched like a drum skin, pulling the bones out of shape.

'That man, the one who killed his wife?'

'Parap?'

'What will happen?'

'I'll take him back and send him to Laiagam for the District Court. Do you want some sweet potatoes, they've been cooking in the fire.'

'No, thanks, I've already eaten. How far is it to the next stop?'

'Two, two and a half days, if the track has been kept up.'

And there is something different about this line tonight, Alec feels it; in the middle men and the old men, even the meris. Today they were touching him again. They didn't normally touch him so much — not any more. When he first came down the valley, almost five years ago, from Karakar, through Poragali and Panduaka, here to Tabunak, they had not seen a white man for eighteen years. They hid in the bush and he waited four days for them to come out. On the fourth day a baby girl stumbled into the clearing and Alec plucked her up and carried her on his shoulders around the camp, singing to her, 'This is the way the farmer rides . . .' until her moaning, shivering mother approached like a hungry animal. The child wanted to stay on the kiap's shoulders and the meri laughed, and the kiap laughed, and the little girl cried. The middle men came after that and then the young men, the children, the women and finally the old men. And they touched the kiap's legs and his hair and his arms and his testicles. The kiap was tall and white and carried cargo of many wonderful, beautiful and dangerous things.

Alone, sometimes Alec would think of the valley. Empty of people — tropical, lush, wet, still and he would place himself in the middle and curl in upon himself. He would not move, only listen. The isolation. The feel of palm leaves and sword grass and the smell of a million years of patient decay and growth. Occasionally a bird call, a lizard's shuffle. Alec would feel that the valley and he shared a secret; a secret not of words. A secret that grew in places fertile of the soil; of the mind; a secret about stillness and people and aloneness and ever and ever.

4

The kiap says I am sixteen, and he writes in his census book that my father and mother are dead from the poison of uncooked pig. He knows almost everything, the kiap. What he does not know is that tonight he will be killed and tomorrow he will be eaten.

I know now that he is the master spirit; the one that Wahgi, in his white clay, sings of by the river; the one who will bring strength and cargo to the line. He speaks of the roads which will bring trucks and the white flower which will bring money. He is the one who brings the future to the valley.

Behind the haus-kiap, the ground sing-sing is filling with those that came in the morning to be counted. Wahgi and some of the other middle men have begun to dance. I watch their laplaps curve in a wave from their bellies to their toes as they rock forward and back together. Wahgi is taller than the others, his drum is more beautiful and he holds it higher so that it moves in rhythm with his body. His body shines with oil through the blue smoke of the fires, and I think he is a spirit-man, of the night, to enter and own the bodies of such as me.

Through holes in the pit-pit walls of the rest-haus, I can see the kiap and the little doctor. I see the white flesh of the kiap's arms and his face. The smoke of our cooking fires has made his eyes wet. He pushes some kaukau into the fire with his boot, and listens to the tanim-tok. The tanim-tok says that he does not like the Tabunak line — that we do not ask about the planting of the white flower, and the work for the roads, like the others at Iumbis and Karakar. The kiap listens.

The ground sing-sing is shaking with the feet of the whole line. They are all here, to eat a part of the kiap and the little doctor. The meris stand close behind the row of young men and make them want to dance stronger. The middle men chew betel nut as they dance, it spreads the black pools of their eyes and gives them dreams of strength as they chant and rock and drum across the night. The sureness of the rhythm is entering us all. I would stand behind the middle men, behind Wahgi. It is forbidden, and I know that I will not, but in my mind I let my breast touch his back and I see him dance stronger; I can feel the heat of him like steam from wet fire stones. And I can see the old women disapprove and pull me back behind the young men — hissing and gaggling at me with their toothless mouths. Inside, I am not shamed for this — for how I feel.

5

The grass packed into Alec's canvas bed sleeve is too much, and wadded too tightly; the young men trying too hard to please. He is awake and listens to the drums and the thudding feet. In the dark he can see the mound that is Edith, face down, asleep before he had finished her shoulders. Lying like that he cannot see her clearly; her hair could be dark and her eyes could be darker. Too hard for a first patrol; she should be back in Mt. Hagen, treading the rows of steel hospital beds.

To be awake late at night had once been a secret pleasure. Thinking was different from daylight moments; nothing was expected, no interruption likely, no possibility too extreme. Tonight is different.

The sound of chanting pulses through the smoke across the sing-sing ground, trickles through the pit-pit walls and stings at him in the dark. He rolls across the canvas bed, dropping his feet to the floor in search of his boots. The reassurance of steel and leather; the power of the Masta; the boots of the kiap. What is different tonight? Outside, the fires are still heaped with giant river stones that will be buried with the pigs wrapped in pandanus leaves. And the singing will continue until the stones pass their heat to the dead pigs. Alec is impressed with the size and number of the stones.

He passes the line of singers. Brown, oiled bodies rippling like watery mirrors, multiplying the fires and smelling the night with sweat and flesh and ancient unnamed demons. The rhythmic beauty of the moment makes the kiap smile as he leaves the pathway and urinates in the bushes. This would be his last patrol, he supposes, before his three-month leave. He will return down south to Sydney, and fill the people-emptiness in him by crushing into trains and shops and cramped streets of hurrying workers; like plunging cold arms into warm pillow innards. And perhaps he will see her floating in the crowds, a darkling feather.

6

I look again through the wall. The tanim-tok has gone and the little doctor and the kiap are speaking. I do not know all of what they say. I wish that Suli would be here to help me. The kiap says he is going to go back to his home when he finishes the counting of the valley. He has been alone too long, he says. The little doctor asks the kiap if there is anyone for him when he goes home. The kiap says that there was a woman. When the kiap says this, I am struck. I look at him closely. His voice has the sound of my thoughts, the yearning, the dreaming. He says that she has dark hair and dark eyes.

I feel the pain of the kiap reach inside me, and I run from the rest-haus towards the sing-sing fires. I sit alone by the fire and I wonder about the kiap — how there could be pain where there is the power to fly into the air and to drive trucks and buy clothes.

Steam rises from the earth where the holes dug for the pigs are warmed by the fires. The river stones at the centre darken from the flames and the ash. When the heat has wormed into the centre of the stones, it will be time to kill the pigs and place them into the holes together.

7

'Masta?'

'Tanim-tok? Is that you?'

'Yes, Masta, I am sick.'

'What is wrong?'

'I am poisoned a little in the belly.'

'Poisoned?'

'The Tul-Tul gave me bad pig.'

'I will wake the little doctor.'

'No, please Masta, I will go to my brother's house at Kandep. He has medicine. I have had the pains before. There is a boy here named Suli, who can turn the talk for you.'

Edith is still asleep as Alec watches her breathing for a while, then leans on the pit-pit windowsill. From the back of the fires and beyond, he can hear the pigs that are tied to sharpened stakes, shrieking and pulling as if the vapours and fumes of their killers and of the stones and the oven holes themselves reek of deathliness.

Once, on a night something like this one, he had written something. He hadn't intended it to be anything, and felt surprised, holding it carefully: a clumsy poem about aloneness. It seemed so small against the night. The sky full of frozen points; a thousand solitary thoughts of a thousand isolated dreams, separate, untouching, slowly melting.

At the closest fire, he notices the young meri who came to

the census table, orphaned, her face down, crying without sound, struggling with what was meant to be in his poem. He smiles at her and nods his head in recognition. He sees her turn away and disappear into the folds of smoke and bodies. Alec would like to talk to her, comfort her somehow, although no way to do this occurs to him. Perhaps, like taro and milk powder, they could trade their isolation.

8

The kiap sees me watching him. He smiles and moves his head at me. I can feel the shame rush from my chest and fill my neck and my face. I want to smile at him but I cannot, I hide my face. I would go to him but I am afraid. I have dark hair and dark eyes. But I run shivering into the heartline of meris. I no longer wish to eat any of the kiap.

Safe amongst the meris, I watch the middle men crack the skulls of the pigs which pull at the cords that hold them and scream and shit and scour the night. One of the grey ones escapes but is caught by the children who fall on it and split its head with their stony fists. I think of the kiap. I know that I must tell him to go now, in the night, before they do this to him.

9

In the darkness, Alec shifts in his sleep on the rough canvas bed and sees: Jack holding his jacket outspread with his arms flapping like wings. He is flying through the air and Alec is encouraging him to fly higher. Anik is clapping her hands and laughing and jumping up and down with excitement. And Jack spirals higher and higher. In the distance Alec can see his father looking upwards, shielding his eyes from the sun with a hand to his forehead, shaking his head in disapproval. Alec's mother is opening and closing her worn hands into fists and out again, into fists and out again. Anik moves closer, touching. She has ceased looking towards Jack. Alec is aware of a faint, flesh-like scent.

10

I run to find Suli to tell the kiap for me. He is not with the other boys or at the cutting of the pigs. I remember Suli by the river, at his man-coming, and his face when the middle men would kill me. I do not think that Suli would help me tell the kiap — and I stop looking for him. I go back to the haus-kiap and look through the wall again. He sleeps above the ground on his grass bed. I remember Wahgi's warning, the scrape of the dried white clay against my body, I know that I must not tell the kiap, but I cannot stop.

Inside the house I can hear the sleeping sounds of the little doctor. My feet make a terrible noise on the floor matting and my body shivers as I strain to see in the dark. The kiap sleeps with a cloth across his body and it rises and falls with his breathing. Outside the squeals of the dying pigs and the children mix together between each drumbeat of the dancers. The kiap turns on his bed. I stop moving and close my eyes. In that moment I do not know why I have come to warn him. I do not know why I cannot carefully tiptoe out of the room and run back to the line. I kneel near the bed. I cannot touch him, my hand will not obey. I wait and let my breath rush across his face.

11

Alec sees her, black in the night; close. Her warm breath eddies across his face. He reaches through the vapour and touches her dark hair. She pulls her head back without thinking.

'Anik?' he says.

She says nothing, frozen by her own recklessness in coming so close to the Masta. He leans his elbows into the bed sleeve, raising the top half of his body, and squints at her. She rises to go but he quickly grabs her hair. She freezes again and wishes she had not come to warn him. She sees the red coals of the fire reflected off the bush knife he has pulled from under his blankets. 'He will cut me now,' she thinks, 'and I am the last of my blood. He will cut me and we will both die; the warning of Wahgi is true.'

He grips the meri's throat with his left hand, the thumb choking off her windpipe. The flat blade of the bush knife arcs above his head. She shuts her eyes and is thrown backwards onto the pit-pit floor, his knee presses into her stomach. The knife descends like a hawk on a scrub mouse and slices into the bamboo at the side of her face. He sees enough to recognise her. Edith wakes and strains to see.

'What is it?'

Alec removes his knee from Koam's stomach and lifts her to her feet by the neck.

'What, for Christ's sake, are you doing?'

She stares at him, speechless, preparing for death.

'Spik pidjin?' he asks. The whites of her eyes penetrate the dark between them. Alec smells her fear.

'Maybe she's sick,' Edith suggests.

'Yu sik?' Alec asks, poking at her belly and pulling a pained face. Koam does not move. 'Tanim-tok's gone to Kandep,' he says to himself. He releases the meri's neck and points at her to remain. He puts methylated spirits into the Coleman lamp and lights it. Koam is shaking. Edith sits on the bed sleeve pole with her sleeping bag clutched around her shoulders. The lamp is pumped into life, hissing its one note.

From the doorway, Alec calls for the Tul-Tul, who arrives sweating and uncertain. He frowns with surprise at the sight of the meri in the haus-kiap.

'Boi bilong misin sikool — tanim-tok,' Alec says, pointing to his ear and then to his mouth. 'Misin sikool boi.'

'Suli?' says the Tul-Tul. The kiap nods and the Tul-Tul shuffles off into the night.

Koam has tucked her hands into her armpits as her whole body shakes. She stares at the steel tricounis on the underside of the kiap's boots.

The Tul-Tul arrives, clutching Suli. He feeds him through the doorway to the kiap.

'You speak English?' Alec says to the boy.

'Yes, Masta, but with some pidjin too,' he says. Suli is shaking and his words come out between deep breaths.

'What is her name?' Alec points to the meri.

'Koam. She can speak some English too, Masta.'

'The meri with no one?'

'Yes, Masta.'

'Ask her what she is doing in the haus-kiap.'

Suli stands close to Koam and speaks to her rapidly in Enga. Koam looks at the Tul-Tul and does not reply. Suli pushes her and speaks again with annoyance. Koam looks at the kiap and whispers softly to Suli. Suli looks quickly to the Tul-Tul and then to the kiap; he is breathing faster. He crosses his arms to hold his own shoulders from shaking.

'Her talk is sickness,' he says to Alec. 'She is longlong.' He touches his forehead and shakes his head.

'What does she say?'

Suli looks to the Tul-Tul with panic. The Tul-Tul laughs and taps his head and staggers around drunkenly. Suli laughs.

'She says that she hears whispering in the kunai . . . in the grasses.' Suli glances again at the Tul-Tul who is grinning back at him. Suli's face breaks into a smile. 'She comes to warn you,' he splutters into his hands with embarrassment. 'That you should not be . . . eating the pigs.'

Suli speaks in Enga to the Tul-Tul, who makes a howling noise of derision and babbles back to Suli.

'The Tul-Tul says she is mad since the dying of her father and mother.'

Alec looks at Koam and sees the anger in her eyes.

'Then she can come back to the patrol post with me. We have a big doctor who comes.'

Suli translates for the Tul-Tul, who shakes his head and replies in a serious tone to him.

'The Tul-Tul says that we must keep her — Wahgi wishes to make marriage with her.'

'Why should Wahgi want to marry a longlong meri?'

Suli looks away from the kiap, to the cut in the floor. The Tul-Tul speaks rapidly to Suli who shakes his head and does not turn the talk for the kiap. Alec is tired and annoyed.

'She will come back to the station with me,' he says. 'There is a doctor who can fix longlong meris at Mt. Hagen.' He turns to Suli. 'Tell her.'

Suli translates the kiap's words to Koam. His face appears tense.

'Masta, she goes to the mission school with me, and knows many English words and . . .'

'She can go to the Government school at the station.' Alec looks at the Tul-Tul. 'When she is better, of course.'

Some would pin upon a God their
wish for immortality. Cold killing
skewers unplucked to plug a leaky
death.
What noise an endless note? Who
sees an unchanged tree? What shall
a God for everlasting ever do?
I say your shape is carved by shoeless
slide on death's honed razor. For
riskless feet that blunt the blade, tread
lifelong danceless streets.

12

New Guinea April 4th 1968

I step into the marks made by the kiap's boots. The little doctor follows behind me. The track is worn by the feet of the traders from Mendi and the pigs taken to graze in the old kaukau gardens. The carriers of the kiap's boxes have gone ahead. Suli has told me I must go with the kiap to be punished at the station. I know that he has not turned the talk straight to the kiap. He tells me that the words I hear are not in the kunai, but in my head. Perhaps the things that I think are madness — the things that I hear by the river — as Suli says, live only in my mind. But I would like to hurt Suli for when he laughs at me with the Tul-Tul, and I feel the ends of my fingers curl with the need.

I am tired from walking but I will not show this to the kiap or the little doctor. I am further than ever before from the places I have always known. They will not see this tightness within me, nor the cold that has come to me with the rain.

In front of me the kiap stops and turns. The rain has filled his boots and made them heavy. I know he watches me even though I cannot look at his face. He says something to the little doctor and then he takes my arm. I can tell that he is shocked at the cold of my skin. He leads me off the path. With his bush knife he cuts at the scrub and vines. He points to big rocks that lie in the side of the hills in the distance. I think that we will take shelter under the rocks. I do not want to leave the track. I am trained by my mother to walk along the worn ruts and to feel the clay uncovered from the loose topsoil by the feet of the line. The kiap pulls my arm to follow him as he splits the bush. The little doctor is close behind me.

The dark will be down before the kiap can cut his way to the rocks. I am too cold and too tired to run past the little doctor and back to the track. I wonder what the middle men and Wahgi would have done with me if the kiap had not taken me with him.

There is an evenness to our steps in the rain — like the pounding to soften taro for the toothless old ones.

13

In the darkening wetness, the shapes of the overhanging rocks are barely visible. Alec stops under the first one. It is shelter from the rain, but the wind chatters around them as they lose body heat from standing still. Alec knows that they will not reach the patrol post at Kandep before it is too dark to see. The carriers have been sent ahead hours ago. He signals the two women to follow as he searches for greater protection. The wind sprays an icy mist up under the rocks as water gutters down the side of the mountain.

Ahead, he can see a deeper hollow, half-hidden by fallen timber and vines. He signals to them his direction as he turns to climb.

The hollow is mouth to a solid rock cave which opens up inside to a larger chamber. He pulls them into the cave and flicks his cigarette lighter into life, holding it at arm's length towards the walls. He feels the walls with his free hand. In one, a round doorway has been worn into the sandstone. He leans inside the hole with the arm carrying the lighter outstretched and gazes at another room. There will be even less wind in here, he thinks. He waves at the women to follow. Koam pushes past the little doctor and runs back towards the opening. The kiap leaps after her, catching her by the ankle. She screams, and swings wildly around and bites into his arm. Alec slaps her hard on the side of the head, jarring her teeth free. He pulls her head back by the hair and bangs her hard in front of her ear with the flat of his hand. Koam wets herself; the urine follows the path of the rain down the leg of the kiap, through his socks and into his boots. He pulls his leg from under her and shouts at her. Koam moans and begins to rock backwards and forwards where she sits. Alec picks her up under her arms and drags her through the door hole.

The three of them lie in the darkness, listening to the heavy breaths of the kiap and the short, sharp, frightened ones of Koam Laman.

With his face close to the floor of the cave, Alec smells something above the stink of urine — the scent of wet animal fur and earth, a reminder of trapping rabbits in his youth. He had trapped them, sometimes with nets and ferrets, sometimes with steel traps. The art was to know the fresh burrow from the old, the one that was still in use. He became so good at distinguishing, he felt he could sometimes hear the thumping heart of the rabbit beneath the ground. It was important to set the trap properly; to use a piece of newspaper correctly placed across the mouth of the trap so a clod of earth wouldn't lodge under the iron tongue or between the serrated jaws when they snapped shut. He could remember the feel of sandshoes with no socks, and the burning in the lungs from running too long to check the traps before anyone had even had breakfast, the wet morning grass soaking through to his feet. And the time that he stopped trapping, when he found just the back leg of a young fox: a blood-blackened stump, chewed off just above the iron jaws.

Somewhere, further in, there is water running and dripping. The blackness is now solid and keeps them close together. Against one wall is a roughly cut pile of firewood stacked in a spiral, pigsty fashion around a centre stake. The stake is supported by a cairn of stones and clay which forms a rough platform for the wood.

'Can we have a fire?' Edith asks, shivering.

Alec feels the wood. It is dry. In the centre of the room there is a circle of small stones holding back a mound of grey and black ashes.

'This is fresh,' he says.

'What do you mean?'

'Someone lives here.'

Alec slices repeatedly into the side of a piece of the firewood, making slithers stand off like a straw broom head. He collects them in a pile and then splits kindling. The two women wait, listening to the reassuring sounds of the craftsman.

The warmth of the fire spreads quickly. Alec watches the smoke coil towards the ceiling and disappear in an updraft. It does not sink down to them again and sting their eyes. Alec is grateful. He feels Koam's shoulder. It is warmer, but she has not stopped shivering. He can see in the firelight her eyes sweeping around the cave. She has the look of the rabbit tangled in the net, held by the trap.

'No food and no blankets,' he says to Edith. 'Some of the carriers may backtrack for a while when we don't arrive at the station, but they won't find us off the track here.'

'Is she all right?' Edith asks, nodding towards Koam.

'I think so.'

'She doesn't look mad, does she?'

14

The fear has not gone from me with the hand of the kiap and the passing of my water. I am not mad. We are too far from the pathway of the line. We are in the haus of Kuipa, the collector, and my mother's stories come back to me.

Kuipa, my mother said, was a boy of the time before her father's father, in the beginning of the valley. He was a boy who would not walk along the tracks of the line — he would leave the safety of the paths and wander into the bush, making his own ways. In the beginning, it was told, he would crawl through the thickness of the scrub or leap from treetop to treetop, and his mother could not catch him, nor could she ever hold him. As the boy became a man, he was met by a masalai deep inside the bush who did to him the things of the night. His flesh and bones were twisted while he screamed, and he was left alone, ugly, a searcher for the bodies of others. And he would wait amongst the thick of the vines and the pandanus leaves and call to the walkers on the track. Calls that could be heard only inside their heads. 'Kuipa calls you, Kuipa calls you to his haus, come with Kuipa.' Calls that were heard in sleep.

Some said he had become a masalai of the night; of the bush. That he made for himself a haus where he led those who would leave the track. That he could slip into their bodies and make them what he wished, or protect them, or set them free.

That he was a collector of men and of dreams — a gatherer for the Tambran.

The words of Suli and the Tul-Tul come back to me. The madness from the dying of my mother and father. The madness which makes voices. Sanguma, sorceress, sanguma, sorceress.

15

In her sleep, Koam has coiled her body against the back of the kiap. He feels her twitching and shaking and cold. He places more wood on the fire and lies close to her with one arm across her body. He feels tired numbness seeping from his neck to his spine to his legs — the swoop of sleep. The curve of her body fits snugly against him; a pleasurable warm comfort. In her sleep, she wriggles closer, and her arm curls across his chest. Alec smiles in half sleep: dark eyes, deep heart.

Past the flicker of fire shadows on the wall, sliding and sweeping across the stone floor, comes the smell of the hunter, a noosemaker, a whorling, threading worm to paralyse and penetrate the flesh of cornered prey. Alec presses closer into the warmth of her body.

Through the doorway of the cave, Alec can see circles of light. Torches burning. The rain must have stopped, he thinks. The circles of light appear to be carried. They move closer. Pulse by pulse, closer. Alec's mind rolls out of dream to reality; the illusion becoming real; the warning of the girl with no one, the longlong meri, weaving through his reason: 'She hears whispering in the kunai . . .

she comes to warn you . . .

she is mad since the dying of her father and mother.'

Alec sits up with a jerk.

Standing near the fire watching him is a man, thin as a shadow. He smiles at Alec's eyes; the flames flicker the white of his teeth against his black skin. His face is deformed and the smile is like twisted wire in flesh. Through the opening he looks to the torchlights outside the cave and back to Alec. Alec wakes Koam and the little doctor. They sit up, half-filled with sleep, and stare at the thin black man smiling his crooked smile at them. Alec lifts Koam to her feet and Edith stands up quickly. He picks up the bush knife. Koam turns to see the flames of the torches outside; she looks at Alec and says in English, 'They come for you.'

The shadow man moves off further into the cave, waving his hand for them to follow. There is no talk as they step carefully behind him, moving further into the cave. Alec holds a burning stick from the fire. In front of him, he sees the feet of the man; his ankles are bent into a U shape so that he walks on the tops of his feet, the soles, pink, untouched, pointing upwards. The man is a leper. Alec has seen it before: warped bones and twisted flesh from years of the disease. And this is the leper's den. Alec can hear Koam speaking softly to herself in Enga. One word from her chanting is repeated many times: 'Kuipa'. Behind them, in the distance, the torchlights have entered the cave. The leper stops at a widened chamber which is the end of the cave. He points upwards on the cave wall. Alec holds the flame higher. He sees nothing. The leper swiftly climbs towards the roof of the cave, his twisted feet easily finding toeholes in the rough stone face. At the top, he turns to smile down at them and suddenly disappears. Koam and Edith huddle closer to Alec. The leper's head reappears. Alec stretches his arm holding the flame higher. The leper lies on a body-length ledge that wraps around itself enough for one person to be hidden. He climbs down. The smoke smell of the torches coming for them moves closer.

The cave tunnels go no further. The leper is no longer there. Alec puts down the bush knife and takes hold of Koam under her arms, lifting her towards the hiding ledge.

He feels her fingers dig into his arms. She shakes her head vigorously and pushes with her feet, away from the wall. Alec lowers her to the ground. He knows there is little time left before the torch carriers are upon them. He lifts Edith, but she is too heavy. Koam takes one side of her and lifts with him. Edith rises up the wall, grasps the ledge and pulls herself into hiding. Alec and Koam look at the space where she has disappeared.

Through the cave, the hunters' chants forge towards them. Alec's flame is almost out. There is nowhere to run. He reaches for Koam's hand. The flame struggles to continue. The girl's hand is strong and warm. In the flickering light Alec can see her face. There is little fear. Perhaps she is not in danger herself, he thinks, and that is why she chooses not to take the hiding place. Alec looks up at the ledge where Edith is completely hidden. He turns to Koam.

'You speak some English?'

'Yes.'

'Are you afraid?'

'Yes, but they will not see it.'

Alec squeezes her hand tighter.

It occurs to him that perhaps he should not hold her hand, that she should not appear to be linked with him, for her own sake. He releases her hand.

'Run back to them,' he says. 'Go on.' Koam looks at him but does not move.

'And they come for me,' she says.

'The boy, Suli,' Alec says. 'He did not turn the talk true, did he?' Alec shakes his head at his own foolishness in not listening more closely to the girl's warning and to his own instincts. Koam grips his hand again. He looks at her small shape alongside him. Her eyes spread wider in the fading light.

The Tabunak men tread silently into the end chamber. They move around the walls sideways, as far from the kiap as possible, the burning torches held in front of their faces. Alec cannot recognise them. Koam's hand grips his desperately. Alec can see axes and machetes tucked in the rough bark belts. One of them steps forward and grabs at Koam's arm. Alec kicks him hard in the stomach. The man cries out, drops his torch, folds forward and falls to the ground. Alec pulls hard on Koam's arm and they begin to run together out of the mouth of the cave towards the lights. And away. Alec wishing himself past the approaching Tabunak line, and down the face of the valley, leaping rocks and fallen trees and breaking through the bush. And Alec waiting to trip and sprawl headfirst, arms outstretched, down the mountain, rolling over and over. Waiting to crack his head against the stony ground, over and over. Waiting for the pain.

Above the pain there is the sound of singing. Deep and warm; the voice of Elvis Presley. And there is flying. Through the air. Jack is flying. In a plane. He sits firmly in the seat of a plane. Jack is coming. Hand in hand, Alec and Koam run down the face of the valley.

Feel the dance
of the mind's wish
stepping firmly,
reeling, twirling:
priceless prints
in unseen soil.

PART III

1

Jack's legs press into the seat in front of him. His body, at sixteen, finally refusing his footballing hopes, is long and skinny. He would like to stretch out across the two vacant seats alongside him and sleep, but he does not want the stewardess who offered to adjust the armrests to see him as a boy.

The plane is quieter and smoother than he imagined, and it is easy to write the letter to his mother. He tells her that he is not flying directly to Paris. 'I am sorry for not telling you this,' he writes, 'but you probably would have stopped me.'

It is totally black outside the plane, Jack can't even see the wings. 'I have sent a telegram to dad,' he writes, 'and I will send you one when I get there, don't worry, I will be okay.'

Without asking, the stewardess raises the armrests on the seats alongside Jack and places a pillow at the end. He smiles at her but is slightly disappointed inside.

2

Grass clippings explode into the air at each slice of the prisoners' sarifs. The long, thin-bladed knives bend like wings through the air. Alec stops halfway up the hill on the way to his house and squats to watch the steady chopping action. Tarus, who has waited until late afternoon to talk to the kiap, sits alongside him, ensuring his head is lower than the kiap's. The sun is beginning to slide down behind the patrol post office.

'Masta.' The tanim-tok looks at the ground in front of the kiap.

'Yes.'

'The meri you bring back from Tabunak — the one with no father or mother.'

'Koam Laman.'

'Here at the station, Masta, there is talk.'

Alec waits without speaking.

'They say that she is for Wahgi.' Tarus's eyes fix on the swinging sarifs. 'And they say more things.'

Alec tries to make eye contact with Tarus.

'They say she is already the kiap's meri.'

'And what do you say to them?'

'I tell them that the end of such talk is the kalabus.'

Alec smiles. Tarus is still agitated.

'Wahgi will come, Masta, he has many pigs and he wishes to buy the meri.'

'I am happy that Wahgi comes to buy the meri, and I am pleased that you have told me.'

'Thank you, Masta.'

'Tell the sergeant to count the sarifs, and put away the prisoners.'

As he approaches the house, Alec can hear the house-cook clanking the fuel stove to make tea. Dark is a half-hour away. It is a time Alec enjoys; the day's work over. In Sydney, at his first job as a junior clerk in York Street, he would stop at the top of the long Wynyard station escalators and stare at the city lights which were just at that moment coming on. His heart would pound with the promises and potential of so many people, so many lights.

3

The kiap's house-cook calls me bush kanaka, and I call her pig mother. She does not like to share her learning of the work in the house, and the words come through her teeth when the kiap is not watching. I wear the clothes of the police wives and the patrol post meris. Beneath the dress, I am covered by clothes so thin and white they do not stop the sunlight. With the clothes of the kiap, they must be washed in his tubs every day, and held up to the sun. I have not been sent to the kalabus. I have seen through the wire fence and I am happy to be in the kiap's house and to learn the work of the house. The kiap pays me with money for my work and I keep it in a tin under my bed.

I have heard talk that Wahgi comes for me, but I do not let these thoughts wallow in my mind. Today the kiap walked to the Government schoolhouse with me, and I am seen with new respect in the classroom.

4

Alec waits at the edge of the patrol post airstrip as the single-engined Cessna carrying mail, Government stores, and Jack rolls to a stop. He does not recognise the tall boy in jeans sitting next to the pilot. From the front seat, Jack smiles and waves. Alec waves back.

A line of kalabus pulls the cargo from the belly of the plane and swings it onto heads and shoulders, like ants tearing at a not-quite-dead grasshopper. Alec watches the silent order and efficiency of the scene as the pilot waits patiently in the plane reading a magazine. The crushed yellow stone of the runway, packed and rolled by hand, is still wet from the afternoon rain. The boy in jeans steps down from the plane and walks directly towards Alec. He stops short of him and they do not touch, but stand smiling at each other.

Like the lifting of a canvas bag of paper mail, Alec's underlife is uncovered in a blink.

'Do you recognise me?' Jack asks. Alec reaches out both arms and encircles Jack. The line of kalabus suddenly stops. The police sergeant watches the kiap in surprise for a moment before waving the line onwards.

'I only have a day, Alec.'

From the kitchen, Koam and the house-cook, Iagap, watch Alec and Jack on the verandah. Iagap, in a whisper, asks Koam if the boy is the son of the kiap. Koam says 'no'. The house-cook does not believe her. She asks Alec in pidjin whether Jack is the kiap's picanini. Alec laughs. Koam folds her arms at Iagap from the kitchen. Alec calls her and introduces Jack to Koam and the house-cook. Koam takes a deep breath and speaks English.

'Good afternoon, how do you do,' she says to Jack. Iagap glares at her, Alec smiles encouragement and Jack blushes. Koam notices his confusion and grins with pleasure. The house-cook strides back to the kitchen.

Late into the night, Alec and Jack talk. Koam can hear the buzzing of words muffled through the walls as she lies in the dark.

'Your father never stopped talking about you,' Jack says. 'He made you sound like Jungle Jim.' Alec laughs. Alec, son of Tom — the yarn continues, he thinks to himself.

'I bumped into him about three months ago — he still remembered me — "the boy with the football," he said . . .'

'How does he look?'

'He's got a bit older, but he looks all right. I didn't see your mother. He said you didn't write very often.'

Jack and Alec listen to the hushed and sleeping New Guinea night.

'I used to think I could come up here and stay with you.' Jack stares into the distance. 'But I didn't know exactly where you were.'

Alec feels the days with Jack and Anik as if they were only minutes away.

'How long has your father been back in France?' Alec asks.

'Two years, mum decided, and me, not to go. We didn't have to anymore — stay together, I mean — since I was fifteen.'

Alec and Jack look at each other for a moment and then turn away. At the bottom of the hill, a policeman's dog is barking at the night. Alec thinks he hears Koam turning in her bed.

'Do you remember that fight I had with Ian Isaacs?'

'When you were wearing his fists out, you mean?' Jack laughs. 'Yes. I don't remember what it was about, do you?'

'No.'

'He really hurt my face — and you kept making jokes. I would have hit you, then, if I'd had any energy left.'

Alec can hear Koam walk from her room and out the back door. He imagines her squatting over the cut grass outside; the inside toilet an impossible taboo to overcome, yet.

'Remember my birthday party when we played that game?'

'Charades.'

'Yes, and we all sat around talking. And the time you took me up in the Tiger Moth . . .'

'And you almost leapt out.'

'I didn't mean to do that.'

'Is your mother happy, Jack?'

'I think so. She likes her work and goes out with someone she works with. Grandpa died about a year ago, but she didn't go to his funeral.' Jack settles back in the cane armchair, looks at the sparsely furnished room: seagrass matting, two cane chairs and a table. 'She said you were like Grandpa.'

'Why didn't she go to the funeral?'

'She didn't talk about that. I think she didn't want him to be gone. Are you ever going back to Sydney? I mean, you could see her.'

Alec listens to the sounds of Koam carefully closing the back door and returning to her bed.

'I *can* talk about the other stuff — you know — what happened to me, and that.'

Alec stands up. 'Would you like some coffee?' Jack nods and follows Alec to the kitchen.

The fire in the fuel stove is still glowing. Alec blows at it, places more wood on and blows again with a thin blast of air like a trumpet player. It was something to do with the high altitude; the thin highlands air, he thinks. Not enough oxygen. He had watched a thousand fires start.

'I think I did mean to do it — you know, with the knife. I didn't mean to hurt him, really.'

A flame pops out at the end of Alec's breath.

'I think I thought it could stop everything — with one jab. It sounds a bit mad. I didn't want to kill him, though.'

Alec turns to Jack and places a hand on his shoulder. Barely visible in her doorway, Alec makes out the shape of Koam, watching; he imagines her dark hair and eyes. Jack's body shivers.

'I told them what happened, like you said — that I thought he was a robber and that he must have tripped or something. But they didn't believe me. They heard you telling me what to say, they told me.'

Alec smiles at Koam over Jack's shoulder. Jack stops shaking.

'Is that why you lost your job?'

'No.'

'Remember in the car that day — when I couldn't stop crying . . . ?' Jack watches the flames held in the iron of the stove. 'I hardly ever cry any more.'

5

Before reaching the airstrip, Alec and Jack climb down to a small creek bed. The old wooden bridge is being replaced with strong new poles. Jack stops to watch. Three policemen and a line of a hundred kalabus, their blue laplaps flapping, have tied lengths of vines to a huge, cut tree trunk. From one side they begin to sing and pull in unison. And inch by inch the mighty tree begins to close the gap. As it nears halfway, the weight on the vines increases. The chanting of the kalabus rises in response to the log's determination to nose down into the gully. Jack watches the vines squeezing into the shoulders of the kalabus. The log stops; the weight is too much. With a smile, Alec runs up the bank and takes hold of the nearest vine. The kalabus laugh with pleasure and point to Alec, who pretends to move the log by himself. There is a cry from one of them, and the hundred bodies fold forward, increasing the strain. The log begins to slide forward. It strikes the opposite bank, showering clay, mud and riverstones, and then with a roar, it is lifted up onto the bank, into place.

The log-pulling has imprinted like film on Jack's mind. The lifting of an impossible weight; a gap too wide; the kindling of a hundred impossible lifters; the log moving, erasing the space, blank by blank. Alec's dream of himself.

In Enga, the kalabus chant how the kiap lifted the mighty

tree. Alec laughs back at them, and leads Jack up out of the creek and towards the flat of the landing area.

Before he climbs into the plane, Jack gives Alec a bundle of papers covered in fine even handwriting.

'I finished it,' he says.

6

With two kerosene pressure lamps hissing on the table in front of him, Alec opens Jack's bundle of papers. Half of them have been torn from exercise books and have discoloured to a creamish pallor, the rest have ringbinder holes and are crisp white. Alec reads the title: *The Two Boys Who Went To War*. He laughs out loud, in recognition, slapping the papers and his hand down on the table. Koam comes to the doorway to see. Alec holds up the sheets of paper.

'This is a story — Jack wrote. He started writing it a long time ago.' Koam smiles and returns to the kitchen.

He reads from the end of the old part, and remembers Tom trapped in his hole in the German P.O.W. camp. Alec shakes his head at the brave, young handwriting. Tom has continued to dig with his pocket-knife into the dirt walls of his prison. Tunnel after tunnel he scrapes and claws and digs, sending the dirt flying out at night and waiting patiently in the day in the cool of his earth pocket. The Germans stop bringing food and the toilet buckets do not arrive. But Tom has been carefully saving scraps of food for months — dried pieces of meat and bread and clay bowls of water. They would not starve him out, and he would never stop digging towards his friend Bill's hole — no matter how much laughter he heard.

The weeks drag into months and Tom digs into hole after hole but always there is no Bill or any other prisoner. Finally there is no food left, and the stench of his own toilet is unbearable. Tom decides to climb out of the next hole he breaks through. If he is shot through the head, then so be it; he is not afraid any longer.

It is a clear morning when he breaks through to a hole the furthest from his own. He digs footholes in the wall and climbs to the fresh morning air. There are no gunshots, no German soldiers and no guard dogs. He turns in each direction, but there is no one, and no sign of anyone. The gates are open, and a wind blows a dry dust through the wire of the fence. He begins to walk, and retraces his own long-ago path.

Exhausted and starving, Tom arrives back at his original post on the front line. Everyone is amazed to see him, and in a daze, he is hospitalised and carried to a ship bound for home.

His family is overjoyed to see him alive and well. They tell him that they thought he was dead. Especially when Bill turned up about a year before and told them about the prison camp. At first Tom can't believe that Bill is alive, that he has escaped without him, without his friend.

Tom discovers that he has grown very strong from all the digging and tunnelling. He is asked to try out for the town's football team, and he does. He quickly becomes a powerful footballer with special ability to penetrate the other team's defensive lines. And it is at a final game that Tom discovers, on the other team, opposite him on the line out, Bill.

Bill is very shocked to see Tom alive. He tells Tom that they all escaped one night and he went to Tom's hole but couldn't find him, he sung out to him and threw clods of earth down to him but there was no answer. Bill and the others decided Tom had died. Tom doesn't tell Bill that he was probably underground, tunnelling towards Bill's hole at the time. It doesn't seem important any more.

The half-time whistle blows and the ball is passed to Tom. He scoops it under his arm and runs for the try line, his boots digging into the turf, spraying soil and torn grass behind him. He sidesteps neatly as if the opposing players are riveted to the ground. Between him and the line there is finally only one player left to stop him: Bill. Out of the corner of his eye, he sees the spectators in their foggy cars rubbing round holes to see through. And there is Bill crouching low, waiting to stop him from reaching the line. The line is very close. Tom leaps upwards in a diving movement, aiming his body over Bill's left shoulder and reaching the ball towards the line. A tooting of car horns rises through the rain. Spectators are waving wet arms out of the windows of their cars. Bill is grinning at him with respect. His teammates are running towards him with pride. Tom leaps high into the air with excitement, and the car horns and the slapping sounds of hands on his back are louder and stronger than gunshots.

7

The rain sweeps in waves of wind across the corrugated iron roof and drops safely into the water tanks. In the dark, Alec rolls onto his back and stares towards the ceiling, listening to the overflow after each gust. He feels calmer, and is pleased that it is so. Before, he would have paced at night. His track, always the same, had left worn prints in the matting. Around the bed, down the hall past the right-side chair, around the table, into the kitchen, and back again. And back again. The heart, Alec thinks, like a child at church, waits for freedom.

Between the rolls of rain, he can hear voices from Koam's room. He sits up in bed, listening. There should be no one for her to talk to. Iagap has gone to Laiagam for a land dispute and will not return for weeks. Koam should be alone. Alec strains to hear. The rain surges and fades. There are two voices. He stands alongside his bed, pulling on his shorts and reaching for a torch. He waits and listens again. The torch points his way along the worn pathway, up the hallway and stops outside Koam's room.

She speaks in Enga. Alec listens, he understands a few of the words. He opens the door and shines the torch into the bedroom. Koam's face appears frightened above the sheet. Alec's heart is pounding. There is another person alongside her, hidden under the bedclothes. Alec strides to the bed and lifts the blankets into the air, tossing them against the wall.

In the torchlight he sees it is a meri. She is Koam's age and stares wide-eyed at the light. Alec is stunned. He aims the torchlight at Koam and then back to the meri. His mind, like disturbed ants, crawls in a hundred directions.

'It is Gabi,' Koam says.

With all his strength, Alec flings the torch at the wall between the two of them. Koam jumps to her feet, standing on the bed. Gabi holds her empty bilam against her stomach.

'Jesus, Christ!' Alec shouts at Koam, his whole body shaking. 'What are you doing?'

'What do you mean?' Koam asks, alarmed.

'You sleep with a meri!' Koam looks at Gabi with bewilderment. Alec continues.

'You go up a meri!' Alec senses Koam's face in the dark, her confusion.

The wind has dropped, Alec hears his own breathing and realises his stupid mistake. The two women are afraid to move. He sits with a flopping action onto the bed, his words falling through the air with the rain.

'It is Gabi,' Koam says again. 'She comes from Tabunak.' Alec leans against the wall. 'Her picanini was born without life.'

He looks at Gabi, picks up the blanket and hands it to her.

'I am sorry,' he says to Koam. 'I am not properly awake, tell your friend I must have been dreaming of the night masalai while I slept.' Koam relaxes her body.

'You do not believe in the masalai.'

'I'm sorry. Tell your friend I am sorry for her baby.'

Koam speaks Enga to Gabi.

'She has run away from her husband,' Koam tells Alec.

'Where is she from?'

'Her family come from Tambul but they do not have the pigs or kina to return to her husband. They say she must stay with him. She has been to the mission and they say she must go back to her husband, and have another picanini, and that her feelings will pass.'

Alec sits on the bed and reaches out to Koam. She does not move as his hand touches her face.

'I have money in my tin, but not enough,' she says.

'How much was paid?'

Koam speaks to Gabi. Alec listens to the rhythm of the talk in Enga.

'It is fifty pigs and one hundred kina.'

'Tell her the kiap will buy this for her.'

Koam looks at Alec with shock.

'Tell her,' he says.

Koam speaks to Gabi. Gabi begins to shake and cry. She speaks in broken words to Koam. Koam leans away from Alec.

'She asks if she is to be your wife?'

Alec shakes his head in amusement.

'No, she can carry stone for the Tambul road.' Koam tells Gabi. Her crying stops. 'Tell her to get back into bed — the kiap's mind is straight now.' To himself he mutters, 'As much as it will ever be.'

Koam watches the kiap's white feet return to his room, each foot falling softly into the matting's past scars.

And the wind on the rooftop continues its dance with the rain as Alec turns in his bed and remembers:

Something about his mother and him. He was leaning against the oven door in the kitchen. It was the year he was at doorknob height. The year he knew that the tiny little scratches on the inside of the toilet door, like the rungs of some insect ladder, which marked the top of his head, made past times measurable and future times inevitable. His mother was holding a book against her chest, and looked out the kitchen window where the whole length of the street stretched. She would watch for hours the life of the street: Mrs. Kane, the widow who ran the two-storey boarding house for gents, and old retired Malone, who dug his garden over and over into dust-blown uselessness, like himself; and Brigitte, seventeen, in tight skirts and lambswool pullovers, who had too many boyfriends for such a street.

From that window she could see Alec's father riding his old bike with the handle bars turned upwards and outwards, tilting like gun barrels. Riding his creaking bike home. At the bottom of the street he would take his hat off to wave to a wife he couldn't always see, but knew was there. His mother was still holding the book when she bent down and hugged Alec. The book pressed into his ribs. They both stared out the window at the street which failed to bring a moving person into view and sat empty in cold winter stillness. Alec knew his mother was crying about something to do with the street and the book and the winter, and the funny feeling even he used to get sometimes when he touched the scratches on the toilet door; the ones stretching downwards like scab-lined, barbed-wire cuts on his legs.

'The name of the book reminded me of something,' she said. 'When I was young.'

'How tall were you?' Alec asked.

'A bit taller than you are now,' she laughed.

Old Malone had come out with his long-handled shovel and had begun digging and breaking clods, never looking up.

'I was going to do something . . . something, one great thing . . . I don't know what . . .'

'Look, here comes dad.'

Gun barrels pointing and hat waving as he moves his weight from pedal to pedal.

'Here, you take the book. I'm going to make your father some scones.'

Alec remembers the feel of the book, but not its title. He takes it to his room and puts it under his pillow for later on.

'I'll do it for you,' he says to his mother as she rolls out the scone dough.

'What's that, darling?'

'One great thing, I'll do it for you.'

8

I sit at the back of the classroom and do not answer questions, I let my mind wander. Many times I have the answer, but I know that the boys already whisper 'sanguma' with my name. The daughter of the police sergeant did not stay in the classroom one day, but ran to her mother's home on the far side of the patrol post when the boys laughed at her. I live in the house of the kiap, and it is different for me, the power of the kiap protects me like a coat against the rain.

Gabi has gone to her one-toks at Tambul and I stay and work alone in the house of the kiap. I know that this should not be, but it is for the kiap to say, and he does not.

I think of Gabi and her baby coming out of her body like stone. A thick silent lump, and inside I weep for the child and for Gabi whose heart is unwarmed and beats so slowly that it fails to flutter the picanini to life. I would like to ask the kiap — to understand about these things.

On some nights I think of how it is said that Wahgi is coming for me. I see him as the clay man, by the river, and his eyes are harder than those of the man who spoke to me in the gardens long ago. I see myself as his wife, with his hands on my body and I think that my picaninis would be born with life, and that they would have the respect of the valley.

The teacher is telling us he will be gone to his house for one hour and we should write from the words on the blackboard.

I like to write words into my books and to read them out

loud to myself when I am alone. Sometimes I try to write words in Enga from their sound but it is a language that resists the kalabus of the page — and needs to run free from the tongue.

The boys at the front of the class have stopped working and are calling out loudly to each other now that the teacher has gone. I continue my writing. One of the boys who has a mission name, Wesley, and another called Peil, the son of a policeman, are standing near my desk. Wesley is the best in the class at English and he is the only one of us who wears sandals on his feet.

'Would you like to play a game with us?' he says to me.

I have never been asked to join with their games and I put my pencil down and stare at both of them.

'I can finish writing your words quickly for you later,' Wesley says. He shows me his book with the words neatly written in rows down the page.

'You write like the teacher,' I say. Some of the other boys in the class are watching us.

'You have to have your eyes covered,' Peil says. 'And then we all move about the room and you have to guess who it is that says, "hullo, Koam" to you.'

'If you get two of the voices right, then someone takes your place,' Wesley says to me.

'Where will I sit?' I ask. Wesley runs to the front of the room and drags the teacher's chair into the centre of the room.

'Here, sit here,' he calls. I move to the teacher's chair and watch the other boys becoming interested. Peil ties a cloth around my eyes.

'Can you see?' he says.

'No.'

'Do you understand, you mustn't look?'

'Yes,' I say, as I listen to moving feet and bodies around me. And then there is quiet.

'Hullo, Koam,' I hear from behind me. I think it is Mapei, but I am wrong and they all laugh at my mistake.

'Hullo, Koam.' This time I know it is Peil.

'Yes!' they all shout. I am pleased I could know his voice.

'Hullo, Koam,' I hear, but it is too soft and I can only

guess. I am wrong and there is much laughter.

'Hullo, Koam.' It is Wesley who has changed his voice to sound like a meri.

'Wesley,' I say, and there is laughter and clapping.

Peil unties the cloth from my eyes and I am laughing with everyone else. My eyes are blinking from the tight cloth and the light. I go to stand up but something is strange, the chair is stuck to me. The whole room erupts with laughter, Peil and Wesley are rolling across the floor, pointing at me as I try to stand with the chair hanging from my dress. I feel my face go hot and I push at the chair with great strength. There is a tearing sound as the chair comes away and I feel the pull of it through my clothing. The chair falls to the floor, free. On its seat, like tiny flags, flutter pieces of my dress, thumbtacked many times to the wood. The air is choked with the sound of boys laughing and whooping out loud at what they see. From inside me, a blackness like staining ink spreads. I step across the room and run to the store shed. Inside, there are tools for the garden and the school. I take the teacher's large bush knife and run back to the classroom. Most of the boys sit back at their desks and point at me, laughing as I enter. I stand at Wesley's desk with the bush knife hidden behind me. I wait until his eyes meet mine and then I swing it from over my head as hard as I can down on his desk. The top splits with a terrible sound. Wesley's scream is like the cry of an injured pig. I swing again and feel the jarring through my arms and up to the bones in my chin. The desk falls into two halves on either side of Wesley's legs. The other boys run towards the door as Wesley screams again, but they do not pass through, as the teacher bars the way. I look at Wesley, who has not been cut and sits without moving. The teacher looks at my dress and at the fear in the eyes of the boys and the anger in my eyes. For one moment he is very still and then he cannot stop himself from smiling. I look at my dress and at Wesley's desk, I do not feel angry any more. The teacher begins to shake his head and the other boys sit down. Wesley stops his noise. I say, 'Hullo, Wesley.' And the laughter starts off slowly and then builds to a roar where even Peil and Wesley and me are caught up.

9

In the middle of the day the air is still, without hint of the cloud that will bring the regular afternoon rain. Alec leaves his office and is drawn by the power of the song unfolding from the bottom of the airstrip and rolling innocently past him. More than two hundred meris tread in rhythmic lines, their netted string bilams sagging with the weight of the crushed yellow stone that will be spilled and pressed to form the extended runway surface.

Alec stops at the edge of the new work and sits on the grass. Many of the women have picaninis perched above their loads, with a tiny leg over each shoulder. The knotted ends of bilams press into their foreheads as they lean forwards as if fighting a great wind. Alec wonders whether the singing is to make the monotonous work bearable or whether it is a product of endless labour: their song in resonant symmetry with a lifeline stretching and disappearing into some imagined point on the horizon.

The men do not carry river stone for the roads and airstrip, nor do they carry food. They will clear the ground for new gardens but will not plant in them.

Except for the stone in their bilams, the meris are echoing the movements of their mothers and grandmothers before them. Stooping and straining; to support, to carry the burden of the line's continuance. Alec watches the oily string cut into their fingers as bilams swing from their backs and empty the brittle, yellow rock onto the ground.

On the hill near his house, he sees Koam moving towards

him, bringing his lunch. She moves steadily towards him, a black shape, sharp against the deep green of the cut grass.

He asks Koam to sit beside him and they eat the heavy bread and dry white cheese, watching and listening. Once, a meri looks up at the two of them and Alec sees Koam meet her gaze defiantly and the meri looks back to the ground again.

Alec points to an older meri with a fat baby on her shoulders. He tells Koam to ask the woman to leave her baby with them while she works. Koam laughs and runs to the meri. Many of the women stop and crowd around to listen. The mother looks up to the kiap and shows her teeth in a wide smile. She lifts her baby by the arms and swings her into Koam's hands. Koam nuzzles the baby with her forehead and nose. With a grin, she steps up to the kiap and passes the baby to him. A whoop of joy goes up from the meris watching. Alec takes the child whose face falls, like a stone in water, through surprise to fear. She begins to cry. The meris cackle with greater delight and slap their hands together, they have never seen such a sight; the kiap holds a picanini meri. Alec takes a pen from his pocket and flicks the spring-loaded button in front of the child. She stops crying and takes hold of the pen. Words in Enga go up from someone close, the meris all howl with laughter. Alec asks Koam what was said.

'She said the kiap has a daughter.'

Alec puts the baby girl onto his shoulders and stands up for all of them to see.

'Tell them, now the kiap is a man of great wealth.' The faces watch and listen closely to Koam interpret. And the laughter sweeps across the airfield and up the valley, overtaking the sluggish, cloud-carrying breeze.

The meris turn together and begin again their singing. The mother of the baby looks back at her child with the kiap as she tightens her bilam for its future load.

The baby holds a slice of Alec's bread and watches him cautiously as she puts it to her mouth.

'Tell me the words of their song,' he says to Koam.

'It is an old song,' Koam says. 'For meris.'

'Can you tell it?' he asks. Koam blushes. She takes the baby and looks towards the meris. Her voice is low and clear.

'It is the story of a meri called Sangu, in the time long before.' Koam looks at the kiap's face and sees his smile of encouragement. 'She worked in the gardens every day, turning the soil and planting. And one day the masalai of the earth, who heard her digging stick, came above the ground to discover who it was that disturbed his world. When he saw the young meri, he knew he was a lonely masalai and he wanted her to stop work and play with him. Sangu said she had no time to play, but the masalai said that he would wait for her to finish her work in the garden. When the meri finished her digging, she loaded her bilam with sweet potatoes and began to carry them to her house. The masalai became angry, but agreed to wait for her. When Sangu emptied her bilam of potatoes at her house, the masalai asked if she was ready to play. But she must make a fire, Sangu said, to cook the potatoes. The masalai cursed and stamped into the earth, sending clouds of dust high into the air. But he waited. When Sangu had made the fire and the potatoes were cooking, she said to the masalai that now she must collect more firewood for the next day. The masalai, in anger, knocked down many trees. But he waited. When Sangu had gathered the firewood, the masalai came close and asked again for her to play. Sangu shook her head, and picked up her empty bilam to carry stones to place around the fire. The masalai looked at her young body with cold eyes, and leaped into her bilam. 'You will carry me,' he said. Sangu refused, he was too heavy, she said. And then the masalai of the earth made himself small, like a baby. 'Now you can carry me,' he said. Sangu looked at the tiny masalai and laughed at how funny he looked, so small. The masalai returned beneath the ground in great anger. There were rumblings and the earth smoked and shook and split in many places. In the night, he returned and found the meri asleep. Through her dreams, he entered her while she slept. And then, when she awoke, she must carry him in her belly, whenever he wishes — whenever he is lonely, and whenever she dreams.'

The baby is asleep between them, her head in Koam's lap and her feet nestled in Alec's hands; the pen has fallen into the grass.

10

Suli, it is Suli coming, and I run to meet him. I feel the Tabunak air has followed him; the smell of the fires and the names of the line. He seems taller and the bones in his chest and shoulders seem stronger. I would like to embrace him but his face, when I am nearer, tells that much of our times together has been lost.

I show him the Government school and the kalabus and the airfield, and I speak to him in English. We sit behind the kiap's house.

'I am going to be a minister for the mission,' he says to me. 'I will be going for special training — to the coast.'

'You will be the first of our line to do such a thing,' I tell him. He likes to hear these words and he holds his head proudly. I am pleased that he has come to talk with me. We have shared many of our days.

'I could not wrestle you to the ground, now,' I say. He laughs.

'And I would still not be able to hold you,' he says. We laugh at the truth in our words.

Before Suli surmounts the sloping walls of Tabunak, there will be many struggles for him: to leave the line. He looks towards the valley and draws his lips together in a line of determination.

'I will come back as a minister,' he says.

At the bottom of the hill, near the patrol post office, the Australian flag is being lowered. I watch its descent in arm-length jerks. As the night hunches deep in the sky, I hear the kalabus returning to their compound.

'Wahgi is coming for you,' Suli says.

'I have heard the talk.'

Suli looks at me closely, for the first time.

'Why did you wake the kiap?' he asks me softly.

I have no answer for him. I have no answer for myself.

Soon the kiap's work will be finished for the day, and he will walk from the office to his house. He will drink tea and listen to music with his radio.

'Gabi has been to see me,' I say. 'She has run away from her husband.'

'No,' says Suli. 'She has gone.'

'Her picanini died, but she will return to her mother,' I tell him.

'She is dead.'

'Gabi?' I say. Suli nods.

'In her house,' he says softly.

'The kiap is to return the bride price,' I tell him. 'She is not dead.'

Suli turns away from me.

'Her picanini did not live.' Suli speaks slowly. 'And she fastened the doors of her mother-in-law's house with logs and pig stakes, and she lit a huge fire which burst through the roof. I could see the flames from my house, above the trees.'

I stop listening to Suli.

'She is going back to her family at Tambul,' I say. 'And she will work on the roads to repay the kiap.'

I see that I am holding Suli's arm very tightly, my finger-nails dig into his flesh. It is a moment that spins my mind and stops my breath, as if I am falling through the air — falling from the face of the valley.

11

Mt. Hagen has informed Alec to stand by for an overseas radio telephone call at 5.30 p.m. It is late. Alec sits in front of the radio, fine-tuning it. Through the office window he has been watching Koam sitting at the rear of his house with someone he feels is familiar. Eventually, Alec recalls the name, Suli, the mission school boy from Tabunak. He watches the body movements as they talk; Koam leaning inwards, Suli angling away.

Hagen Central calls. Alec responds.

'Hagen–Kandep.'

Kandep–Hagen. Call from Sydney, Australia for Glover.'

'Yes, speaking.'

'Connecting now, Kandep.'

'Alec?'

'Yes?'

'It's Anik.'

'Anik.'

'Yes, Jack wrote to me about you.'

'How are you, Anik?'

'Good, Alec. Jack wrote that you look very much the same.'

'Jack seems terrific.'

'He is, Alec, I miss him already. He will be with his father for a few more months and then he will be coming home.'

'We talked a lot while he was here.'

'Yes, he told me in his letter.'

'I was impressed with his daring — coming here, I mean.' Laughter. 'And his organisational ability.'

'My only good genes . . .' Laughter.

'I have missed our conversations.'

'I have too.'

And a thousand thousand unshaped seconds.

'I'm sorry about your father.'

Silence.

'Jack said you may be coming back soon?'

'Yes, soon.'

'Will you come to see us?'

'Of course.'

'Did you see how tall Jack is now?'

'A basketball player.'

'He is very happy, now, Alec . . . and . . . very sensible.'

'I could see that.'

'We still talk about you, you know.'

'Kandep–Hagen, would you finish now, please.'

'Anik, they're going to cut us off.'

'It would be lovely to see you again, Alec.'

'And you.'

'*Au revoir*, Alec.'

'Goodbye, Anik.'

Like unseen threads of the night
spider, love's lacing strands
cling strongest at first
face-brushed shock.
And at the moment before
they are no longer there.

12

In my dream, Gabi is running again down the mountain. Behind her follow the twisted feet of a shadow man, dragging and scraping through the stones and dirt. Around me, like lighted splinters, are held many hundreds of burning torches. Gabi runs towards me with her swollen belly. The torchbearers throw their flaming sticks into a soaring heap in her path. Gabi stops and looks at the shadow that pursues her. She looks to me, and I reach out for her. I see her follower stop and his eyes find me. Gabi runs swiftly, silently, into the heat of the fire. She does not call out as the blaze sends hundreds and hundreds of tiny sparks skywards, lighting the darkness. The shadow man beckons me, and I am afraid. The torchholders pick up their flames and spread through the night around me. I follow Gabi's pursuer into darkness, his strange feet marking a passage. I see him ahead, moving towards the mountain, towards a face of solid rock and I hear the flame carriers treading behind me. At the wall of stone I watch him slowly disappearing, sucked of his shadow, passing through the stone, becoming less clear with the light of the torches. But I cannot pass into the stone, there is something holding me, pressing my arms. I turn into the face of the clay man.

For many hours I lie awake with the dream pressing on top of me. My skin sweats, and I know that I can be alone no longer. The bed is damp from my fear. I move quickly from my bed and follow the path of the kiap to the door of his room.

There is one window, high up in the wall, through which moonlight, the colour of pencil shading, softens the shapes of the room. He does not move on his bed. I know that he is awake and that he watches me. I am not afraid of the kiap, as before. I am afraid like the rock lizard who runs to hide in the darkness at the shadow of a hawk. But the night, like a shadow, is nothing — has no shape, no body, it leaves no trace. And perhaps it is this that I run from.

'Koam?' It is the voice of the kiap and I lie near his body, against the night.

13

Alec turns onto his side to face Koam. Her skin is warm and moist in the humid night. He has listened to her footsteps coming down the hall and watched as she paused in the doorway. She lies on her side, facing him. His face almost touches hers. Alec lifts his hand to her shoulder. The smooth round shape nestles comfortably in his palm, his fingers grip tightly.

'Are you afraid?' he asks. 'A nightmare?' He folds to her shape, touching the length of her body.

'I dream of Gabi,' she says. 'And a fire — and a shadow who passes into a wall of stone — and burning torches that come for me. And the shadow has twisted feet, and I follow him, but I cannot. I am held by a clay man.' Koam holds close to the kiap. 'The clay man is Wahgi.'

In the ancient light, Alec can see the side of Koam's face. His fingers trace and retrace a pathway where light pushes dark.

'I am sanguma,' she whispers.

'No,' Alec says.

'I would not go to my opening at the time my body was ready — when Mennen and the others . . . . Suli says I am too strong for a meri, and I go to school like a boy. And I stole a pig.'

'You stole a pig?'

'From Kaio — and I kept it hidden in the bush and it fed from my breast. I am sanguma. My father and mother die on the one day.'

He strokes her shoulder gently; her forehead and cheeks and neck.

'And Gabi comes to me but Suli says she is dead — by her own fire. And I do not understand.'

Koam speaks more softly, and holds onto Alec tightly.

'I have seen by the river,' she says. 'I have watched the man-coming. I have wanted knowledge that does not belong with me. I have waited in the grass and I have learned that the middle men are jealous and afraid of the bodies and blood of meris; the bodies that can carry life. That they bleed themselves to become greater than the meris and their own fear. And I no longer want this knowledge.'

Alec holds her closer. He marvels at the courage of the girl. He can feel her body shaking as she speaks.

'Wahgi covers himself in clay and he speaks to them. He speaks of eating the body of a man of strength who comes — and the spirit of such a man will breathe on for them.'

Alec would like to pass through her skin, to curl inside her, to calm her fear, and to feel safe. Her body is smooth and slightly damp. Alec touches her gently with his fingertips as she continues.

'I do not know whether my father would be angry with me. He did not want a meri, he wanted a son. He said I was much more. He was a strong man whose thoughts were passed to me like gifts, and I wish that I could speak with him.'

'Perhaps more than a son, your father wanted one with the strength to carry his thoughts.'

Koam raises her head to look at Alec's face. She strains to see in the half-dark. 'What would he say to you now?' Alec asks.

Koam stares at Alec as she thinks.

'He would say that the strength of my wish to know has taken from me as much as it has taken from the middle men. He would say that the things I wish to know are like the pigs of a rich man — in their use, is their loss. He would say that to know the truth is enough.'

Alec kisses her gently on the lips. Koam is surprised. She

frowns in the darkness, touches Alec's face, leans over him and kisses his lips in exactly the same way. Alec realises she has not been kissed before.

'You are a beautiful meri,' Alec says.

'I am a beautiful woman,' Koam says.

Alec laughs. 'My father would call you, "a bit of a girl".'

'What would your father say to you?' Koam asks. Alec thinks of his father and smiles to himself. 'He would say — I never should have come to this country in the first place . . . and that it reminds him of the time he went droving . . .' Alec laughs. '. . . And my mother would ask did I ever do that one great thing.'

'And the woman with the dark eyes and dark hair . . . ?' Alec is surprised that Koam could know of Anik.

'She is called Anik.'

'Anik,' Koam says. 'She is like me?'

'Yes,' Alec says.

'The boy, Jack, he is your son?'

'No,' Alec says.

In the distance, from the far side of the patrol post, Alec can hear voices calling out. He is surprised that any of the police or warders or others would be still awake. A gust of wind rattles a loose piece of roofing iron. Koam kisses him again. Alec's head moves over her body, his mouth cooling and soothing. Along the line of her neck and shoulders and breasts. Across the round of her stomach.

'No!' she says, as she holds Alec's head firmly in her hands. 'It is poison. I am in blood, moon blood!'

Alec gently takes her hands away from his face and moves between her legs. He tastes the sharp, salty edge of her blood, and draws it warmly inside him.

14

Wahgi stops short of the patrol post land. The group closest to him, of middle men and young men, sit and make jokes to him about his power with women. The young meris and children sit at a distance, waiting for the wives carrying babies to catch up. The men smoke bush tobacco and point towards the kiap's house at the top of the hill. Wahgi does not speak to those who have chosen to follow him from Tabunak, uninvited, but inside he is pleased. It is a sign of his importance, a sign that his life is larger than any of theirs.

This marriage is different from his others; the meri, Koam, is different. He remembers her touch from behind at the sing-sing, and how she would never run from him like the others; and how the Tul-Tul could not stop her from going to the mission school. And how she woke the kiap. He would need to hurt this one. Wahgi stands and the group follows, climbing the kiap's hill.

15

Tarus waits for Alec to finish giving instructions to the police sergeant. Alec is his fifth kiap and the tanim-tok often feels the 'softness' in the belly of this one. It meant less respect, less fear from the bush kanakas and the workers — and a harder job for the tanim-tok. The softness, Tarus believes, comes from letting them inside; the weaker ones, feeling their pain and anger. It would run around inside and bruise the blood. Sometimes Tarus would not turn the talk straight, he would add 'iron' to the kiap's words and the result would be better, Tarus's name depending on the strength of the kiap as a meri depends on the strength of her husband. He feels that the kiap might know his thoughts; the kiap who is soft in the belly, but whose mind and words are straight and clear.

The sergeant nods to the tanim-tok as he leaves the office. Tarus waits for the kiap to notice him.

'Masta.'

Alec looks up from his desk.

'I have been asked to talk to you by the Tul-Tul from Tabunak,' Tarus says. Alec can see that Tarus finds difficulty in speaking to him on matters that are not work-related.

'They say that you should receive Wahgi, who has come for the meri, Koam, that you should stand for the meri's father, and set the bride price.'

'What do you think, Tarus?'

'There was a part of the line of her mother's brother, but they have gone from Wabag to the coast.' The tanim-tok is embarrassed by the kiap's focus on his opinion. He does not want to have one. He does not approve of the girl living in the house of the kiap.

'I think, who will stand for her, Masta, if you do not?'

16

I see them as they begin to climb the hill. It is easy for me to recognize Wahgi. He is at the front. I am surprised that so many have walked from Tabunak to watch. The sight does not move me as I once thought it would. I had dreamed of Wahgi coming to me and how we would be together. As I watch them climbing, growing larger, I wonder what it is that has changed. So many of my wishes, like Gabi's baby, are born unmoving into a real world.

Perhaps it is me that has been changed — with the learning of things that should not be known, and new words to hold them.

From outside his office, I can see the kiap stand and beckon to Tarus to come with him, as he too moves towards me.

17

Alec can see the kina shells and necklaces neatly laid out in rows in front of Wahgi where he sits, his legs folded, his wig a black triangle imitating the mountain background. Alec guesses there must be three hundred men, women and children sitting patiently on the lawn facing his house. He tells Tarus to speak with the Tul-Tul as he enters the house in search of Koam.

He moves slowly through the house, the chatter of the expectant crowd outside following him from room to room. Koam is not in the kitchen or in her room. Alec opens the back door and looks in all directions. There is only his own bedroom not searched. He moves surely down the hall.

Koam stands in the centre of his room, facing the only full-length mirror in the house. For a second Alec watches, and then moves to stand alongside her. Both stare at the reflection of themselves. Koam smiles and Alec's reflection smiles back.

'Tarus has asked me to stand as your father, to bargain with Wahgi,' he says. Koam's duplicate frowns.

'Will you do this?'

Alec watches the two of them together: real and shadow, each an imitation of the other.

'No, you are the one . . .'

'A meri cannot.'

'I will be with you.'

'They will not listen.'

'I'll tell them that you are standing for yourself, and for your father.'

Koam's image moves closer to the kiap. Alec attempts to speak, to say what he has come to know about Koam Laman. But he is aware that the moment in which they stand in front of the mirror, with Wahgi waiting, a voice away, is as shatterable as glass. Together they turn from the mirror to face each other. They smile and Alec leaves.

In front of his house, Alec nods to Waghi. Tarus comes to wait by his side.

'Tell them, welcome to the ground of the kiap,' he says to Tarus. The tanim-tok waves an arm expansively as he speaks in Enga. A murmur of approval moves through the crowd.

'I have been asked to stand for Koam Laman's father,' Alec says in a strong voice which skims above their heads.

'In the bride price talks with Wahgi Kumin of Tabunak — and I have said, "no".'

Without hesitating, Tarus interprets the kiap's words. Alec makes eye contact with Wahgi.

'I have spoken to the meri, Koam, and it is she who will stand for her father and for herself.'

Tarus looks shocked, but quickly turns the kiap's words. For half a second there is silence and then the group erupts. A shrieking comes from the old women at the back, the middle men babble at Wahgi, three old men leap to their feet. They shout abuse at Tarus, as if he had not spoken the true words of the kiap. Wahgi speaks to Tarus and the noise pauses.

'Wahgi says that a meri cannot do this, Masta.'

'Tell Wahgi that there can be no marriage bargaining, then — the meri has no one.'

Tarus's neck twitches, he breaks his own code and speaks back to the kiap without turning the talk.

'Masta, Wahgi would lose face in dealing with a meri.'

'Turn the talk, Tarus.'

Wahgi does not move when he hears the kiap's words, he does not look away from the kiap's eyes. It is this courage that has made him wealthy, Alec thinks. From the back of the group a wrinkled old man curses and mumbles; stepping over the seated bodies on his way to the front, he bends and begins to collect the kina, pausing to wave them threateningly at Tarus. Wahgi stops the old man and speaks to Tarus.

'Masta, Wahgi says that if you were to sit alongside the meri, then the words could be from both herself and her father.'

Alec turns to see Koam through the window. He signals to her to come to him. Wahgi watches her move to the kiap. He sees them speak to each other and the kiap sit alongside Koam on the highest step to his house. Several of the old men and women rise and curse at the others around them. They pull at the arms of those around them to get them to rise and leave. As they fail, they spit and hiss towards Tarus and hobble down the hill, their shouting becoming braver and softer with distance. A matter of pride: Alec remembers the old bum in the park so many years ago — abusing his charity; preserving a past that might perjure the future.

Wahgi addresses Tarus. Tarus becomes nervous and speaks Enga back to Wahgi. Koam looks at Wahgi and then to the kiap.

'What does he say, Tarus?' Alec asks.

'Masta . . . I am not sure.' Tarus looks at Koam and then down at the ground.

'Turn the talk, Tarus.'

'Masta . . .' Tarus shifts his position. 'He says . . . that he must make sure . . . before the talk . . . that the meri is not . . . has not . . . that the kiap . . . that the meri . . . is not the woman of the kiap.'

Alec stands up on the step. Tarus does not wait for the kiap. He quickly tells Wahgi that the meri cooks for the kiap and cleans his house. Wahgi replies to Tarus.

'Masta, Wahgi says that she should leave the kiap's house, if he is to make marriage with her.'

'Tell Wahgi his words are the talk of a man who hides himself behind clay to frighten small boys.'

Tarus's eyes go wide. He looks with panic to Koam.

18

I rise to my feet alongside the kiap. I can see the top of Wahgi's wig: the saved black hair, carefully shaped to add to his height. My mouth is opening and words come out as if I watch a mirror that returns the outline of someone else. The faces of the crowd are turned towards me. I do not make the talk my father would have made, but my words carry to all those present.

'Wahgi, who comes to make offer for me with his kina and pigs, must first examine what he would buy. He must weigh the risk that he takes if he inspects only my body and trusts that what he cannot see is unchanged. Like the sleeping snake, there is much to be wary of:

I have stolen the pig of Kaio Pagaip. I have felt the death of the picanini of Gabi Lekun, and I have dreamed of the shadow man. I have heard the mystical forest bird, whose feathers hang from the body of a middle man. I have watched, by the river, a boy become a man with blood from his nose. I have seen the strength of the line, not poison, flow through the blood of its meris and feed its children. I know that what Wahgi has come to buy is in the glass of his own mirror.'

My talking has stopped. There is silence. All of the kina and gifts have been gathered up and the marriage group is trailing away down the mountain. Some of them turn and shake their fists and spit towards me. Except there is one young meri who has listened to the end, and who smiles at me before she runs to catch up with the others.

Yearn not for a sure and certain
mind, as the balanced scale, in
a world whose only test for life
is motion, need not ever move.

19

Alec sits opposite Koam. She pours tea into his chipped mug, and they both enjoy the certainties of breakfast movements together. Outside, the fog has not yet lifted, and dampens any sound of the waking patrol post.

Koam has talked long into the night with the kiap, about her own words to Wahgi and the difficulty in understanding the changing picture that is herself.

Alec turns the bread toasting on the kerosene stove. He leans across Koam's back to reach the plate and feels again the pleasure of touching her. He lingers with breakfast and waits to wipe the dishes. There are few words between them. Koam insists on placing each dripping plate and cup into his hands. They laugh at the game they play to finish each item first.

Alec lights a cigarette and watches Koam move about the room. He wants her to ask to walk with him to the patrol post office.

In such moments, Alec begins to recognise the depth of his past isolation like an illness understood only as one begins to recover. He would like to express this to her — the difference she makes — but words, he knows, have lives like picked flowers. And she will be here when he returns today: an uncut bloom.

Halfway down the hill, Alec turns and waves to her as she stands at the window.

The office has not been unlocked, and Alec is surprised that the police sergeant or Tarus has not been to collect the keys for the kalabus. He uses his own key. Inside, he notices that the patrol post key-ring is gone. He imagines that they must not have been returned last night, and makes a mental note to reprimand the sergeant.

It is almost time for the 8.00 a.m. radio call to Mt. Hagen to report the rainfall and airstrip condition. He flicks the switches and automatically tunes the frequency knob. The sound crackles faintly — the charge indicator needle points to the red. Alec curses with irritation, disconnects the battery and realises the replacement has been used in the truck. He connects the flat battery to the charger and starts the diesel engine generator.

With the engine noise driving him from the office, he heads for the bottom of the airfield. There is no water on the surface of the strip, and he is grateful, even though the Government stores plane is not due for three days.

At the end of the runway, he can see no one — no line of meris or supervising policemen. Perhaps they have moved to another job, he thinks, but no likely place occurs to him. Alec switches direction towards the kalabus compound on the other side of the patrol post. His steps lengthen.

Across the runway, jumping the deeply-cut drain, up onto the road and past the neat policemen's houses. Alec notices that there is no smoke from any of the houses; there are no children playing in the front gardens or on the grass footpath. Alec stops. There are no sounds of people anywhere. There is a stillness — not a leaf moves.

Alec strides along the roadway, his boots rolling and stumbling on riverstones too large at the edge of the road. Ahead, the prison compound comes into view; the high, barbed-wire fence, bent at the top, impossible to climb over; a jagged scar on a soft green face. And closer. Alec is breathing heavily, his hands grip around the wire. The gates are open, and the wind blows a dry dust through the wire of the fence.

Up the green hill, with the toes of his boots tearing the grass. And at the top, a view of the patrol post. And no movement. In the distance, the schoolhouse.

Down the slope, heels slipping, knees locking. And closer. Across the road, jumping the drain, running through the playground. And pulling at the door.

Alec stands, his body squeezing tiny drops of sweat from every pore. The darkness of the classroom slowly lightens, and there in her seat, alone, sits Koam Laman.

20

In the truck, Alec tells Koam that he does not know where everyone has gone. He stops the vehicle outside the sergeant's house; the door is unlocked and Alec walks through the rooms. He places his hand on the top of the fuel stove and there is no warmth, no recent fire. He would make a joke about public holidays or visitors from outer space, but Koam would not understand.

They drive again around the patrol post roads and look inside houses. And further south, to the last of the stoned section, where the road becomes a track. There, in the mud, trailing away down the valley are the marks of moving feet.

Towards the centre of the roadway, Alec notices deeper heel marks made by boots; Government boots supplied to patrol post police and warders. Surrounding them, as if from cattle herders, lie the shapes of hundreds of bare feet.

'This is the way that Wahgi and the others returned to Tabunak,' Koam says.

Alec inspects the mud again and considers whether it is possible that all of the patrol post inhabitants could have been rounded up and driven off by the Tabunak line. He turns to Koam knowing that she would read the signs. She waits for his reaction. Alec struggles to think of a reason why the Tabunak line would do such a thing. Revenge? Anger? Payback? Something else? Tarus and the sergeant would never willingly leave the patrol post without seeing him first. He smiles at Koam, who comes to stand close to him. Alec smells the faint flesh-like smell and touches her arm.

'I will have to follow them,' he says.

The track is uneven and littered with pockets of black mud and grassy lumps that hide rocks. In the cabin of the truck, Koam and Alec are bumped and shaken from side to side. Under the seat, Alec has placed a rifle and six cartons of ammunition. He has calculated the amount of fuel they can use, to leave enough to get back.

Alec has stopped trying to find reasonable explanations for what has happened, and even why he is following muddy footprints down the valley. There was no decision made that Koam would be with him. He looks at her watching the track and wonders whether he should ever have brought her back with him from Tabunak. Last night she spoke to him about her life at Tabunak: about Suli and Mennen and Gabi and others; about her father, and things she had seen. She could laugh. She said, 'Once, with Suli, we covered a pig in paint and feathers and leaves and waited for Kaio along the track to the mission school. And when he came, we hid amongst the trees and called with our voices inside a drum, while the pig ran towards Kaio. And he ran, screaming of the piece of forest that pursued him — and Suli and I laughed until the water ran down our faces.'

Alec smiles at the remembered sound of her laughter. He told her some of his father's yarns — about life on the farm — and she understood and laughed as happily as Alec ever had.

The track narrows, and the scrub and branches tear at the sides of the truck with a scraping sound. Alec stops.

'We can't go much further,' he says. He steps down from the vehicle and waits for Koam to get out. He takes the rifle, a box of cartridges and an aluminium flask of water.

Ahead, the track becomes a thin, muddy line. Koam follows behind Alec, carrying the flask. It is mid-afternoon and Alec knows they have less than four hours before it will be too dark to return to the truck. At the edge of the track, in a small clearing, they stop. Stretching beyond is a view of the entire valley. He takes her hand, helping her to stand near him on a sandstone rock. Alec cannot resist calling out, a long joyous note to reach the ears of anyone in the valley and to tell them of his coming. He feels the closeness of Koam and tightens his grip on her hand.

21

The fingers of the kiap interlock with mine and I am pleased. He calls out across the valley — a happy cry which fills me as much as the valley with well-being.

I do not know where the people from the patrol post have gone, but there is a feeling that, like rain on leaves, they have gone with the rising sun. And the kiap and I are also drawn.

22

In the distance, further along the track, Alec can see movement. He strains to see more clearly, and indicates to Koam. The bushes along the track are moving, off the path and away from them. Alec stands higher on the rock. He loads his rifle and watches. With Koam behind, he moves quickly away from the path in pursuit.

There is little time to check the marks along the way and Alec listens for the sound of movement ahead of him. He glances behind regularly to check that Koam is keeping pace. He winds slowly down the face of the valley, a long way from the regular pathway between ground sing-sings. Alec is not sure why he is following so intently — there seems no way to turn back. As always the regular beat of his footsteps through the bush becomes a seductive rhythm; an end in itself.

He knows the afternoon rain will come soon, but it does not matter. Branches of shrubs and trees cling at his arms and face. He is careful not to let them swing into Koam. He turns to reassure himself and stops suddenly. Koam, watching only her feet as she follows, bursts into him and they fall to the ground. Alec holds onto her, laughing. He remains lying on the ground, looking at her. Koam does not try to rise. Over Alec's shoulder, high up in the rocks, she sees movement. She points. Alec can see a black arm waving to them, from a fallen tree, high up in a deep hollow off the track.

As if they are the body of one person, they rise together and climb upwards.

23

Upwards to the hollow which is mouth to a solid rock cave. Alec looks at Koam and knows that she recognises the cave. He hesitates under the rock ledge and, still holding her hand, steps through the opening. Inside it is the same as before. He feels along the walls with his free hand and locates the worn hole that leads into the inner chamber. There is a small fire burning at the far end. He moves to one side so that Koam can see. Alec remembers her fear from before and the scent of wet animal and earth and urine. Beside him, Koam lets go of his hand, reaches up to hold both sides of the opening and pulls herself through. Alec immediately follows.

In the flickering firelight, he can see the neat spiral of firewood stacked against the wall on its platform. And near the fire, the deformed feet of the leper.

24

I see him standing on the other side of the fire. It is Kuipa. His feet are twisted. I know that he is Kuipa, the collector, from the stories of my mother. I am not afraid. I feel again the hand of the kiap.

Near the fire, I sit and can see that the bones of his face and jaw are so misshapen that no words can escape his mouth. I am unsure why I have no fear. I have seen in the old ones that fear grows strongest from a shrinking heart.

The shadow man rises and signals us to follow him further into the cave. He stops, and smiling at the kiap, as if to remind him, he climbs swiftly up the wall and disappears.

25

Alec's heart is thumping and his head hurts. Through the doorway of the cave he can see circles of white light. They move closer. He takes Koam's hand. The leper climbs down from the wall and moves off into the shadows. Alec realises he has brought only the bush knife into the cave with him.

The Tabunak men tread silently into the end chamber. They move around the walls sideways as far from the kiap as possible, the burning torches held in front of their faces. Alec cannot recognise them. Koam's hand grips his desperately. Alec can see axes and machetes tucked into the rough bark belts. One of them steps forward and grabs Koam's arm. Alec kicks him hard in the stomach. The man cries out, drops his torch, folds forward and falls to the ground. Alec pulls hard on Koam's arm and they begin to run together out of the mouth of the cave towards the lights.

Three solid bodies leap onto him. The heat from one of the torches burns his face as they hold him down and struggle to control his arms and legs. Alec's hand with the bush knife breaks free and swings upward into the weight of bodies. The thick wooden handle strikes a ribcage and a cry of shock and pain echoes through the cave. For a second

Alec has the option of plunging the knife into the neck of the heaviest of his attackers. He pauses. In his mind he sees the blade enter the man's throat and the spray of blood. The eyes of the man meet his. Alec recognises the face of a middle man from the Tabunak census. In that moment Alec sees more than terror in the man's eyes as he watches the blade coil back in Alec's free hand. The man sees his own death. He opens his mouth to cry out. Alec waits. And the moment is lost. Two arms fly to his wrist, pinning it back against the rock.

Both his and Koam's wrists are tied with bush vine. They are dragged, bumping and scraping painfully, across the stone floor and out of the cave. They are carried to a flat, cleared space of ground above the cave. Here the torch carriers number in the hundreds; the smoke is thick and there is no singing or dancing, only silence.

Some of the men speak excitedly in Enga. Alec asks Koam what they are saying.

'They look for the little doctor,' she says.

One of the men, covered completely in white clay, moves towards Koam. He carries a heavy trade store machete. He stops in front of her, raises the knife and swings its blade, flat side down, onto Koam's head. Koam flops sideways into Alec from the weight of the blow. Blood from a small wound on her scalp leaks onto Alec's shirt. The clay man stops in front of Alec. Alec coils his knees towards his chest and lashes out with his boots. The steel tricounis chop into the flesh of the clay man's legs. He screams with pain. There is a shocked mumble from the encircling group. The clay man moves in a wide arc behind Alec and swings the blade down flat on his head. Alec slumps further against Koam's body. The pain in his head is sharp and dizzying. He watches Koam sit up and the clay man kneel in front of her with one hand beginning to squeeze her throat. Koam's eyes appear to swell and her mouth opens, desperately struggling for air. The clay man's grip tightens. Alec wriggles himself sideways, preparing to kick out again, but two men grab at his feet; one pulls an axe from his belt and chops at the laces. The blade cuts through the tongue of the boot and slices into Alec's foot. He cries out. The men stop in shock for a second at the sound of the kiap, and then, reassured of his helplessness, tear off his boots and woollen socks. They hold them in the air above their heads and for the first time the crowd roars with excitement. The torches wave wildly in the air and move in closer. In the middle of the clearing, Alec can see two large piles of earth — dirt from very deep, freshly dug holes. Near the holes, and in the fire, are head-sized riverstones, heating.

With a great effort, Alec lashes out with his bare feet, striking the clay man on the side of his face. Blood from his cut ankles and feet sprays across the white clay and onto Koam's head and shoulders. Free of the clay man's grip, she gasps for air. The clay man pulls up a fist-sized stone from the ground and strikes Alec hard on the base of his skull. Alec feels the sharp point of pain and falls across Koam, spinning and giddy. He feels the rock strike again, a dull thump, but there is less pain. There is the sound of singing. In the distance. And an outstretched sprawl, headfirst, over and over.

Behind his back, Alec's left hand begins to pull free as the thin bark of the green vine holding them cracks and splits. The clay man with the bush knife is nowhere in sight; the torchlights appear to have blurred into a single white glare. Alec's left hand wrenches free of the vine, taking several layers of skin. Keeping both hands in place he moves close enough to the girl to begin working the vine around her wrists backwards and forwards with his fingers. The Tabunak line sing in the distance. The soft green vine bends, splitting the bark but not the core. Alec tries to clear his vision by blinking rapidly and screwing up his eyes. Against the light someone approaches. Alec squints into the glare and works frantically at the vine. The shape in front of him stops. It is the leper. The vine snaps. The leper lifts Koam to her feet as Alec rises to follow. His head spins in a dizzying swirl. He feels the rock held by the clay man strike again. And he can no longer not cry out. The sound skittering through the circle of his killers and embedding deep in the marrow of their bones.

PART IV

1

Edith follows Tarus up the side of the mountain. The bush is much the same as she remembers except for the track, which has become considerably more used and is now wide enough for two people to pass.

Tarus is heavier and slower in his movements but he remembers her face. He does not talk during the climb but turns to see if she is keeping pace, as it is obvious she is not as strong as before.

As they reach the cave, surprisingly, Edith does not feel the old fear — the fear that paralysed her as she lay hidden in the ledge — the fear that had come back to her year after year, late at night. Only after telling the story over and over did the nightmares recede.

She had heard that someone had marked the spot some years ago, 'marks in the stone' the locals called it, and she had wanted to see it for herself.

She shakes her head firmly at the tanim-tok when he pauses at the cave entrance. Tarus turns away and climbs upwards to the cleared space above. Edith pulls her way up and sits panting for breath in the clearing. The bush has been creeping into the flattened surface for some years and it is obvious that before much longer there will be little trace of its existence.

Tarus points to the rock wall on the high side of the clearing. Edith squints to focus. Carved into the rock face is a large smooth area covered in neatly chiseled letters. Edith moves close to the rock wall and reads.

In memory of ALEC GLOVER
and KOAM LAMAN who, on
4th April 1968, in this
place, gave their lives
to save District Nurse
Edith Carpenter in an
attack by local tribesmen.

— Jack Pendraud, 1982.

2

High up on the valley wall, Alec turns to Koam as they sit together above the cave and listen to the singing. The singing tells of a new story that will be told to the children of the children of the valley:

> of Koam, the meri with no one, and the kiap who leaves his own line to bring the future; of how they gave strength to the valley; of how the little doctor disappeared by their magic. How at the joining of their blood, their dreams together were too strong and would not die. The story will tell of Kuipa, the twisted one, who collected the runaway dreams of the kiap and Koam, and returned them to the cave.

And the words will be passed through the listeners into the future.

3

The valley in the early evening is still wet from the afternoon rain, still smoking from mist that shivers droplets onto the kiap's shoulder and down his collar.

'I will show you everything,' Alec says to Koam.

They run down the face of the valley, as the kiap tells Koam how they will fill themselves with people in the cities, and of the strange and beautiful cargoes he will show to her. So close together that like the air and the sky, between them there is no line.

Weep not for what seems lost,
for the heart need not return
to that which it never left.

For I am the Master of the dream
and leave to you, dear caretaker,
these prints in the valley.